Dwight Yoakam

D0650953

AMERICAN MUSIC SERIES
Peter Blackstock and David Menconi, *Editors*

DWIGHT
Yoakam

A THOUSAND MILES FROM NOWHERE

Don McLeese

UNIVERSITY OF TEXAS PRESS ❧ AUSTIN

*The publication of this book was supported in part by the
Brad and Michele Moore Roots Music Series Endowment.*

Requests for permission to reproduce material
from this work should be sent to:
  Permissions
  University of Texas Press
  P.O. Box 7819
  Austin, TX 78713–7819
  www.utexas.edu/utpress/about/bpermission.html

The paper used in this book meets the minimum requirements
of ANSI/NISO Z39.48–1992 (R1997) (Permanence of Paper). ∞

Design by Lindsay Starr

LIBRARY OF CONGRESS CATALOGING-IN-PUBLICATION DATA
McLeese, Don.
    Dwight Yoakam : a thousand miles from nowhere /
Don McLeese. — 1st ed.
          p. cm. — (American music series)
    Includes discographical references.
    ISBN 978-0-292-72381-8 (pbk. : alk. paper)
    ISBN 978-0-292-73781-5 (e-book)
    1. Yoakam, Dwight. 2. Country musicians—United States—
Biography. I. Title. II. Series: American music series (Austin, Tex.)
    ML420.Y63M35 2012
    782.421642092—dc23 [B]   2011042859

For Danny Roy Young and Sir Douglas Sahm.
Let's play two!

Contents

Dwight Yoakam

Introduction

A Thousand Miles from Nowhere

LONG BEFORE I COMMITTED myself to this project, which would become a labor of love—an opportunity to immerse myself in the music and rediscover the multidimensional richness of it—I considered Dwight Yoakam an artist of singular accomplishment. Though there are mainstream country artists who have sold far more than the twenty-five million recordings that Yoakam claims, no other has reached those commercial successes by following anything close to Dwight's elevated career path; he has taken artistic chances, attracted a diverse audience, and garnered critical plaudits from the rock world.

On the other hand, while there may be alternative-country, roots-rocking, and kindred-spirit artists who remain revered beyond the mainstream, none can match Yoakam's combination of uncompromising vision of musical integrity and level of popular success. Whatever promises about forging a

common spirit for rock and country have been made by cult favorites such as Gram Parsons or Lucinda Williams—or Jason
and the Scorchers, or Joe Ely, or dozens more who have found
a wellspring of creative revitalization in roadhouse tradition—
Dwight Yoakam has fulfilled. In spades. He has somehow become the most formula-defying popular artist in the most
formula-dependent genre of popular music.

So, there are two questions that a book such as this should
ask and perhaps even answer. Why hasn't anybody else been
able to do what Dwight has done—use a traditional-roots-
alternative base as a springboard to multiplatinum mainstream popularity? And why hasn't Yoakam been celebrated
more for the singularity of his achievement?

Various terms have been coined to describe the musical
chasm that Yoakam straddles: country rock, cowpunk, roots
rock, alt-country, insurgent country, No Depression, et al. The
conundrum encountered by artists who fall into that divide
has always been "too rock for country, too country for rock."
Yet rather than compromising or diluting his musical impulses
at the extremes, Yoakam has pushed the envelope.

When he jumped from the L.A. roots-punk circuit into the
national spotlight, he was too *country* for contemporary country, and he rocked with an unbridled intensity beyond most
contemporary rock. It's fitting that he first attracted notice
among the roots-punk firebrands, sharing fans at Los Angeles
clubs with the likes of the Blasters (whose Dave Alvin was one
of his first important champions), X, and Los Lobos.

Those who saw him in those formative years insist that
they knew even then that not only would he be a big star, he
would be a *mainstream country* star. Whether at the shitkicking
Palomino or the punk-rocking Club Lingerie, even if the crowd
was no more than a dozen or two, Dwight displayed the chops,

charisma, and vision that would command large stages of halls filled with country fans in just a year or two. Heck, it was practically the same set.

His musical progression in the years since has reinforced his singular spirit. Where he initially sounded like the most retro of artists—a hillbilly, honky-tonkin' anachronism with one foot in the 1950s—he soon established himself as a visionary unbound by era, an artist who could title an album *Tomorrow's Sounds Today* and mean it.

He accomplished all this during a period in which contemporary country has become a euphemism for "soft rock," a musical territory where Yoakam's harder edges will never fit. While today's country owes more to the Eagles and Fleetwood Mac than it does to Hank, Merle, and Loretta, its fan base continues to self-identify as country. Go to a country concert and you'll find it dominated by those who listen to country radio, buy country CDs (or download country cuts), maybe even join fan clubs for country artists. They rarely find much of interest on the other side of the contemporary pop-rock divide (and even less in the hip-hop and gangsta rap that have come to dominate pop).

Yet when Yoakam's music was played, primarily, if not exclusively, on the country airwaves, his concerts would attract plenty of fans that never listened to contemporary country radio and rarely went to other country concerts. His artistry was not merely covered but featured and championed in rock publications such as *Rolling Stone*, which typically paid scant attention to mainstream country.

Many of the artists who might be considered Yoakam's contemporaries—such as Steve Earle, Joe Ely, Rosanne Cash, Lucinda Williams, and Lyle Lovett—some of whom were initially marketed as mainstream country hitmakers, now often reach listeners over the airwaves of National Public Radio. Yoakam no more fits there than a honky-tonk bull in a broadcasting china shop.

As I began my initial research for this book, I was blindsided by a couple of revelations. The first is that there has never been any previous biography of Yoakam or book-length study of his music, not even a glorified fan-gossip quickie. This book was intended from the start to be more like an extended piece of music and culture criticism than a comprehensive chronicling of Yoakam's life. It offers lots of analysis of and context for Yoakam's artistic progression, and little to nothing of what Sharon Stone said about him, what veejay Duff thought about him, or what his high school teachers remembered about him. Yet I was pretty amazed to find the field of Yoakam biography wide open, to discover that even at the peak of Dwight's celebrity and commerciality, no one had tried to capitalize on his popularity with a book.

By contrast, the life of the late Gram Parsons, whose legacy looms large decades after his death despite a career that was commercially negligible—certainly in comparison with Yoakam's—has spawned a half dozen biographies (as well as prominent appearances in other books, where he is discussed as seminal inspiration for the shift the Byrds made toward country-rock, a buddy to Keith Richards of the Rolling Stones, and a mentor for Emmylou Harris). Do a book search for Dwight and all you'll find are songbooks, sheet music, and a collection of lyrics printed as poetry (and titled *A Long Way Home*, which is an album title I would have considered borrowing for this book if Yoakam hadn't already reappropriated it).

Another surprise awaited when I searched the archives of *No Depression*, the magazine where I long served as a senior editor and which covered the alt-country movement more comprehensively (and, dare I say, more incisively) than any other publication. Expecting to find at least one extensive career piece on Yoakam, if not a spate of cover stories, I was dumbfounded to discover that there was nothing beyond short album reviews.

The archive gives no indication whatsoever that Yoakam is one of the most commercially successful and artistically compelling musicians to emerge from the movement that also spawned *No Depression*, which was supposed to be the genre's bible. In the pages of *ND*, Dwight had been treated more like an afterthought than a standard-bearer.

I don't mean to bite the hand that fed me (cheese and crackers, but still) or to criticize the editorial acumen of my friends Grant Alden and Peter Blackstock, the magazine's co-founders. (And I should acknowledge here that Peter was responsible for bringing this book to the University of Texas Press. Thanks again, Peter.) They were committed to drawing attention to artists deserving a whole lot more of it, and maybe they felt that Dwight didn't need the help—that he was already too popular to classify as alt-country (whatever that is). And there were always issues of timing, access, and other contenders competing for cover stories. But I'd counter that such a huge hole in *No Depression*'s archives—it's as if *Rolling Stone* had all but ignored the Rolling Stones—suggests that it's quite possible for an artist who has received platinum albums and critical raves to remain underappreciated.

Which raises another question: Why? I'd be tempted to say that the big gulf between Yoakam's achievement and the acknowledgment of it is inexplicable, but the writing of this book suggests, if anything, that there are too many explanations, a confluence of issues that are complex, contradictory, confounding, and often tinged with irony. There are considerations of authenticity, purity, persona, the essence of country music, and the calculations of the music business (a business that some alt-purists treat as if it shouldn't exist) that are easier to raise than to resolve.

So let's preview some issues that we'll more fully explore in the following chapters:

His popularity. There is a prejudice that if that many people like him, especially that many country music fans, he can't be that good. While the whole roots-trad-alt-country corral is filled with mongrel music, there's no purist quite like an alt-country purist. (Except maybe blues purists—self-appointed Caucasian arbiters of what qualifies as authentic black expression.) And when an artist or a band finds greater popularity and wider renown by stretching their creative wings—be it Dwight Yoakam or Wilco—they face a backlash from those who once championed them, many of those fans (in Yoakam's case) strongly believing that anything that's on mainstream country radio must be dreck. Or at least compromised.

From the very start, Dwight Yoakam has approached the music business as a business—one that he has done his best to outsmart, one in which he has pursued commercial success—and he has never claimed otherwise. Purists see failure to achieve such success as a merit badge of musical integrity and a sign of their own superiority of taste. The fact that Yoakam has moved more units than so many artists of the alt-country movement *combined* confirms to some that he sold his soul to Devil Commerce.

Yet Dwight came of age when some of the best-selling music was also the best: the Beatles, the Byrds, the Stones, Creedence. Even Elvis. And his formative country influences were hitmakers all. Limiting his ambition to cult fandom was never part of the game plan.

His authenticity. When Yoakam began drawing raves in the Los Angeles alternative press, it was almost as if he were a coal-dust baby, born to country music, as innocent to big-city ways as a latter-day Beverly Hillbilly. And there's no question that Yoakam played the part and reaped the rewards, as the press emphasized his birth in Pike County, Kentucky, while downplaying the facts that his family had moved to Columbus, Ohio, before he turned two and that he'd briefly attended *The Ohio State University* (as Buckeye natives call it) with interests in philosophy and history before heading west to find a career in show business. They also often failed to mention that he'd been just as involved in theater as he had in music in high school, and he earned a role in a Long Beach stage production before hitting the Southern California bar circuit.

Despite his occasionally exaggerated drawl and a name that seemed to combine "yokel" with "hokum," Yoakam is nobody's rube. He wasn't a backwoods '50s hillbilly but a media-savvy child of the television generation. It's instructive that when I asked Dwight about early musical inspirations, he quickly mentioned the Monkees, the ultimate pop fabrication. Yet watching the Monkees on TV was a far more "authentic" musical experience for a ten-year-old Ohio child in the mid-1960s than listening to Hank Williams and Lefty Frizzell.

Purists might denigrate Dwight as a poseur, which is rockcrit French for "phony," but he's far more authentic as a sum of his influences and inspirations, a reflection of his place and time, than a retro anachronism could ever be. And the growth he showed with albums that would employ strings, horns, and background vocals reflected an artistic expansion that restricting himself to musical anachronism would have denied. The results, on albums that are Yoakam's most creatively ambitious, are timeless in their surrealism, like a honky-tonk dreamscape as directed by David Lynch.

So, why are the 1940s and 1950s inherently more "authentic" than the 1980s and 1990s? And didn't that cowboy hat make old Hank Williams himself something of a poseur?

His performing persona. He had one. From the start. Even if only a few listeners were in the bar, barely paying attention, Dwight looked sharp, and his band played sharp, unlike so many other acts that took the stage as if they'd just rolled out of bed and had barely bothered to tune. Despite some of the places he played or the crowds who supported him, there was never anything vaguely "cowpunk" about Yoakam except the live-wire intensity of the performance.

As Yoakam become more popular, it became increasingly apparent that female fans liked him a lot. This meant male critics felt compelled to make some reference, usually disparaging, to his skintight jeans and twitching butt, which he turned toward the audience too often for the comfort of some. Though sexuality has long been a driving force in popular music, males tend to find qualities with such appeal to females to be spurious, suspect, all sizzle and no steak. (As if the meatiest steak couldn't also sizzle.)

I learned this lesson instinctively before I knew anything about popular music. My babysitter in the mid-1950s loved Elvis Presley, so I instinctively felt compelled to dislike him. Not because I had a thing for my teenage babysitter, a decade older than me, but I perceived that attraction as some kind of threat. Whatever girls liked, especially that much, was yucky.

Dwight has always stressed the necessity of putting on a show. A flashy one. One that would drive the girls wild. Just like he'd seen Elvis Presley do. On television.

His Pete problem. No successful musical artist has ever done it on his own. There is always a manager, producer, bandmates—maybe all of the above—who deserve a share of the credit. Yet with Dwight, his crucial collaborations with guitarist-producer-bandleader Pete Anderson present a particular challenge in the credit-where-credit-is-due department.

Was Pete equally responsible for Yoakam's success? Or more responsible, a sonic Svengali pulling the strings? Dwight had the songs, the voice, the look; Pete had the chops and the sound that would showcase the artist at his best in both the studio and onstage, elevating the role of lead guitar as the singer's essential musical foil. Before Pete, Dwight's career lacked momentum, and his music lacked both edge and focus. The creative tension in their partnership sparked some sort of magic that neither has (thus far) been able to replicate on his own.

Nine years older than Yoakam, Anderson definitely served as a musical mentor. But they suffered a bitter split following 2003's *Population: Me*, when the guitarist sued the singer for lost revenues after Dwight decided to recoup some financial losses by touring without a Pete-led band. Neither has discussed the other much in print since then, until now.

Even so, when I started this book, Yoakam's camp would have preferred that I didn't talk to Anderson, fearing that whatever account he might provide would stir controversy, drawing the wrong kind of attention in order to spur sales. I assured them that I had no intention of writing a book exploiting any tension between Dwight and Pete. And I haven't. But Dwight himself made it plain in our interviews just how integral Pete had been to his musical development, and it would have been journalistically irresponsible to try to tell this story without attempting to incorporate Anderson's perspective.

Ultimately, Dwight and Pete, interviewed independently, had little that was negative to say about each other, and both expressed considerable pride in the music they'd made together. They collaborated for a couple of decades, almost half a lifetime in Yoakam's case. Plenty of marriages don't remain as vital for nearly that long. But, as one of Dwight's songs puts it, "Things change."

So, just as a biography of Elvis Presley must encompass Colonel Tom and a book about John Lennon needs to include Paul McCartney (talk about your bitter splits!), this is a book about Dwight Yoakam—how his music originated, how it has progressed, what it has accomplished. And it's about a legacy that doesn't stop here, for the artist has too many ideas and too much ambition to rest on his laurels for long. Like a lot of those who follow Yoakam—critics and fans alike—I eagerly await the next chapter.

How Far Is Heaven?

IT ISN'T UNTIL AN HOUR into what was promised to be an interview but instead became a monologue—wide-ranging, stream of consciousness, fascinating and frustrating in equal measure—that Dwight Yoakam leaves the conference room of his business office and returns with an acoustic guitar. One that badly needs tuning. And at this point our interchange morphs into something like one of those *Behind the Music* specials.

The setting: the headquarters of Etc., Etc., the nerve center of Dwight's career, located on the fourth floor of the Sunset Boulevard building of the Directors Guild of America. The rectangular table with the marble top flanked by office chairs could pass as the meeting place of any board of directors. Yet the gold and platinum records and the movie posters covering the walls attest to the nature of this particular business—and suggest that, for Dwight Yoakam, business has been good.

The panoramic views of Sunset Boulevard below and the Hollywood Hills above reflect the sense of privilege that success bestows. The vista from a different angle extends all the way downtown, when you can see through the smog. By the window is a telescope through which perhaps Yoakam can view Venus or Mars on a clear night. Nearby are a globe and the *National Geographic Atlas of the World*.

No, from here you can't see Pike County, Kentucky, the mining region that the Yoakam family continued to call home even after moving north to Columbus, Ohio, when Dwight was two. But the real question is whether Dwight could somehow have foreseen all this back then. Could he have envisioned his career in West Hollywood, even some approximation of this office, when he decided to make music his life while still living in Columbus?

Attesting to an artistic vision that extends beyond country traditionalism, or even music, a number of coffee-table-sized art books are stacked in the conference room: Dalí, da Vinci, Warhol. And beneath one of the two speakers, a skull. *Alas, poor Yorick!* Amid the immortality of art and the infinity of the universe, here's a reminder of the end that awaits us all.

The "Etc., Etc." on the outside door of these offices provides an oblique reminder of Yoakam's early recording days, when he released an indie EP in 1985 titled *Guitars, Cadillacs, Etc., Etc.* He quickly became a national country chart topper after Warner Bros./Reprise signed the roadhouse renegade and had him expand the disc into an album with the same title and added a colorized version of the original black-and-white cover. His first full-length release with national distribution turned Yoakam into an overnight sensation, and it had only taken him a decade or so.

The funny thing about the EP and the title is that it wasn't until the expansion into the LP that Yoakam was inspired to write a song called "Guitars, Cadillacs," with "and hillbilly music" replacing the etceteras. (In other words, the EP's title preceded the LP's title song.) His record company initially balked, fearing that the Kentucky-born artist's evocation of what the label considered trailer trash was like waving a rebel flag at the possibility of crossover mainstream success.

But Yoakam stood his ground and "hillbilly music" remained his categorical description of choice (and "crossover" an epithet). Yet the "Etc., Etc." was more than a placeholder in the EP's title. It suggests the inner workings of a mind that sees connections everywhere, generating possibilities without boundaries, where "and so on, and so on" is the sort of transition that can leap chronology and linear logic as well as subject matter.

Start talking with Yoakam about seminal inspirations and you're as likely to hear him wax rhapsodic about the Monkees and the continental shift of television from New York to Los Angeles, thus blazing the trail for his eventual pilgrimage, as you are about the Stonewall Jackson and Johnny Horton influences that made their way from his parents' albums from the Columbia Record Club into his own music.

Hours later, ask him about the breakthrough stage of his musical development in Los Angeles, when he was embraced by the roots-punk crowd before establishing a fan base in contemporary country. Then sit back and roll tape:

"Oh, yeah, that was our crowd. We'd moved out of the brilliance of the '60s, and by then we were into the *Tusk* world of Fleetwood Mac, and nobody knew where it was going. It was over under sideways down.

"We were too country for rock and roll and too rock for Nashville. Pete [Anderson, Yoakam's longtime producer, guitarist, and bandleader] and I had gotten fired from a lot of places, because we wouldn't play that *Urban Cowboy* cover stuff. I used to be on the phone seven hours a day. I booked us. And I had records in my El Camino—the EP—and I'd be driving 'em all over town.

"I was the generation that had given us punk. If I'd gone to New York in '75, '76, it would have been CBGB. What we had was the emotion. When we'd do "Please, Please Baby," the affinity they felt for us at the Whisky a Go Go was like, *holy shit*. They had a lot of rockabilly out here. When I first got here I saw Robert Gordon at the Whisky a Go Go, and he had Link Wray with him. 1978. And Billy Zoom's rockabilly band opened for him. And the Blasters were really rockabilly in a sense. We had the greatest affinity with the Blasters and Los Lobos. Again, guys who were more professional in their execution than Rank and File or Texas Chainsaw Massacre.

"But then Del Fuegos was an interesting band. The Plugz became Del Fuegos when the cowpunk thing started happening. Southern California has always been more of a free-association environment. The Byrds happening alongside Arthur Lee and Love. Go from Paladin and Westerns on television.

"So, we were certainly distinct, but the access point was the emotional reckless abandon. We were as rabid as anyone, it's just that we stayed in tune. And it was shocking to see bodies slamming. It was crazy. We were *slammin'*, but we were in tune! Watch the Beatles on bootleg video, and, man, they were good! Listen to them sing 'Nowhere Man' live, and it was raw, but man, they were the Beatles for a reason! [Dwight starts singing 'Nowhere Man.'] 'Paperback Writer,' wow. What they're doing, they're doing. Those four had depth.

"And when you listen to the Roxy Theatre [recording], that bonus disc with the deluxe edition of 'Guitars, Cadillacs,' *that is the moment!* We knew! We didn't know what we knew, but we knew . . . And maybe we knew that before I realized we knew it."

Not to get all Watergate about this, but what did Dwight know? And when did he know it? Before I began working on this book, one journalist described him as "one of the smartest people in the business," while another warned that he is "too smart for his own good." How come? "He can talk himself in and out of things like five times in one conversation," came the reply. "He's an enigma, man. And God can that guy talk!" That journalist told me about having his own broken jaw wired shut when he first interviewed Yoakam, and how it hadn't made any difference. He wouldn't have gotten a word in edgewise anyway.

One of the many contradictions that makes Yoakam such a provocative artist is that his loquacious reality is so at odds with the brooding image of the noir cowboy who keeps his visage hidden beneath his cowboy hat and his thoughts to himself, preserving that lip curl for his singing. He's a flamboyant, even electrifying, performer, but one never gets the sense that he's revealing much of himself beneath those flashy outfits, with jeans so tight they seem painted on his swiveling hips.

Away from the stage, Dwight has no such flash or airs. And he has no qualms about revealing himself as a balding guy with a few wrinkles and a bit of a paunch—more the character actor that he has become (memorably and menacingly in *Sling Blade*, *Panic Room*, and other roles) than a leading man. Hiding nothing, he holds nothing back. Of all the artists I've interviewed, only the late Doug Sahm (Sir Douglas Quintet, the Texas Tornados) ranks with Yoakam as a world-class talker. The difference is that Doug was more of a memoirist, a one-man oral history project whose sudden shifts had their own logic (sometimes only a logic discernible by Doug, but still). Dwight's mind is more analytical, even philosophical, as he frequently seems to be heading down five different speculative highways at ninety miles per hour, divergent directions on different bridges, all at once.

When preparing for our interview (I'd last talked with him decades before, for a newspaper story), I had dozens of questions covering his formative years in Kentucky and Ohio, his early attempt to launch a career in Nashville, his subsequent struggles and triumph on the West Coast, the progression of his music, and the development of his film sidelight . . .

After an hour, when Dwight leaves to get his guitar, we are on question two. He wasn't out of grade school, let alone high school. But he had written his first song, at the age of eight, and he wanted to play it for me. And this performance provided the key to everything, unlocking the contradictions between sincerity and sham, authenticity and contrivance that lie at the heart of not only Yoakam's music, but of country music in general.

Because when the fifty-four-year-old Yoakam starts singing the first song he had written, he isn't pretending to be eight years old. But his voice has as much sincere innocence in its conviction as a child's. For the minute or so that it takes him to sing that first verse, he is living that song, just as he had when he wrote it.

The song sounds like it should be titled "How Far Is Heaven?," and it's about a little boy who was Dwight's age when he wrote it. The boy's dad was a soldier, killed in Vietnam, and now his father was in heaven, or so the boy has been told. And since the boy, more than anything, wants to see his daddy, he asks the question that obsesses him.

While tuning for maybe ten or fifteen minutes—the guitar itself has become an obsession, and a distraction, as we try to sustain a train of thought in the interview that now threatens to jump the rails—he jokes about his instrumental range: "I haven't gotten that much more sophisticated, for better or worse, but I knew enough to tell that was Johnny Cash," he says of the melodic model for his song.

Finally the strings are close enough to tuned for him to tolerate, and he starts singing with the purity and passion that might have marked his performance if we were in a concert hall holding a few thousand. Or if he were in that boyhood bedroom, alone.

"There's a few things that I don't understand," he sings, his voice plaintive and on the verge of heartbreak. "How far is heaven? When can I go? I miss my dad. Oh, I loved him so."

His voice has the ring of truth, for these are the questions an eight-year-old would ask, maybe even one who hadn't been raised in a fundamentalist church that preached that every word in the Bible is literally true and that heaven is a place far more real than West Hollywood could ever be. A kid that age could only be consoled by the possibility that his dad wasn't gone for good, that the two of them could still reconnect. If only someone would show him the way.

I later read in an early newspaper profile that Dwight had given the song a more prosaic title, befitting a kid his age when he wrote it: "My Daddy Got Killed Over in Vietnam." By whatever title, the song is an invention, a creative fabrication. While the emotional investment of Dwight's performance of the material made it ring true, his own dad wasn't dead, hadn't even served in Vietnam, though he had been a soldier. Dwight had learned about the war the same way he'd discovered practically everything else that would have such a significant impact on his musical persona—from television. And TV was real, a heightened reality.

"I was watching the news all the time, and this is what was on," explains Yoakam, who continues with a critique of his first songwriting effort. "It's not that complex, but how many eight-year-olds would write that? Is heaven a place? From a kid's eye view, it is."

"It's an awfully sad song," replies his lone listener.

"It *is* sad," he agrees. "I walked downstairs and my parents said, 'What are you playing up there?' And I played it for them, and they went, 'What the hell!' They were freaked out. 'There's something wrong with the kid,'" he laughs heartily. "Yes, I was given to invention. But only loosely. 'Cause my dad had been a soldier for awhile.

"I hadn't been seriously writing, but now I knew I could do that. That was a song! At eight years old. My parents looked at me a little weird. *Bizarre*. Not sure what you do with that or what that means. And they had me play it for some friends. And *they* thought it was weird."

The experience left Dwight sure of two things. That he was gifted enough to write songs of his own, songs that would give him control of his artistic destiny. And that he was weird. Maybe those are the same thing, or at least they were to a kid who continued to feel a little bit different all the way through high school in Columbus, Ohio, into his brief stint at his hometown's Ohio State University, then to Nashville, where he didn't fit at all. And finally, maybe inevitably (or so it seems in retrospect), he headed west, to a dream factory where a lot of creative misfits come to reinvent themselves, or to invent themselves in the first place.

Over the course of the rest of our interview, Dwight continues to strum the guitar, letting his thoughts trail into riffs, documenting the chronology of his career through a series of acoustic performances—sometimes an intro and a line or two, sometimes even a whole verse and chorus. But the more that he lets his music speak for him, the less he amplifies upon it. After extending an excursion through the memories of his first eight, largely pre-musical, years into more than an hour, he compresses a summary of his last two decades into little more than thirty minutes, complete with impromptu soundtrack.

He can talk expansively, as if he has all the time in the world, but he's also a restless man with a short attention span.

As the following chapters will show, when he analyzes his songs with specificity, as he did above, the underlying theme of his musical creativity relies more on the abstract. Truth or concoction? Purist or poseur? A throwback to an earlier era or a visionary offering of *Tomorrow's Sounds Today*?

"You don't have to live it to write it," he explains about the writing of "It Won't Hurt," one of his classic honky-tonk ballads about drowning your sorrows in alcohol, which Dwight had never drunk. But he'd played enough bars to internalize what he'd seen. "You write *from* what you know. And then you write *beyond* what you know, *from* what you know, *vis-à-vis* what you know . . . It's the tool that allows the writer to move beyond yourself to something larger than yourself. That's the task at hand. And that's what the best writing can be—using what you know to think beyond yourself."

Are you sure Hank done it this a-way? (I'm pretty positive Hank never said "vis-à-vis." Though, as Chuck Berry might have put it, "'Vis-à-vis' say the old folks. It goes to show you never can tell.")

The "real" Dwight Yoakam may forever remain an enigma, as complicated as any of us, more complicated than most. But his music is as real as it gets. It delivers a truth that takes something from the facts of his life but uses that literal factuality as a seed, a springboard, a launching pad. So let's call this a musical biography of Dwight Yoakam, a book about the life of the music, for the creative truth of the art is almost always more significant than the factual truth of the artist who made it.

2

Readin', Rightin', Rt. 23

IN THE EARLY SONG that best reflects Yoakam's creative authenticity, his ability to render the details of a life that seemed so different, so exotic, so *real*, to fans and fellow musicians in Los Angeles—yet were more a projection from his life than a reflection of it—he sings, "They learned readin', rightin', Route 23 to the jobs that lay waiting in those cities' factories. They didn't know that old highway could lead them to a world of misery."

The "they" in the song are those schooled in the coal mining country of rural Kentucky, just south of the Ohio border, where the third of the three Rs was the road out of town. The most important lesson kids learned in the schools of Pike County was that they needed to leave it far behind if they hoped for something better from life than a coal coffin.

Though that version of the three Rs was a familiar joke in Pike County, Dwight was never one of those kids. His perspective on Route 23 ran north to south, rather than vice versa.

Kentucky wasn't the place he'd hoped to escape, it was the home to which his family returned, pretty much every weekend.

The "world of misery"? That would be Columbus, Ohio, a hundred miles or so to the north on the twisting, two-lane Route 23. Not that far, but a whole different world: a big city rather than a rural county, where emancipation from the mines meant the blue-collar drudgery of the assembly-line factory. In other words, pick your poison.

Yet by Dwight's own account, the life that he lived with his parents in Columbus, Ohio, where the family moved before he was two, was far from miserable. He was a reasonably happy kid in a reasonably happy household. But the family missed Kentucky and had close ties to relatives there, so practically every Friday they'd pack up the car, hit the road, and travel south to Pikeville. Whenever they talked about "goin' home," it was understood that "home" meant Pike County.

That route would provide the lifeline for Yoakam's music, the return to Pike County giving his artistry the sort of richness that those heading the other way hoped to find in the material world. Long before he had settled on a career ambition as a country musician, he knew that "in some way, this part of the country would be at the heart of whatever I would do," he says. He lived in both worlds, never completely leaving one for the other.

Thus, "Readin', Rightin', Rt. 23" is a more complex song in terms of perspective than it might initially appear. In his collection of lyrics, *A Long Way Home*, Dwight follows the song with this dedication: "Written for and lovingly dedicated to my mother, Ruth Ann; to my aunts, Margaret, Mary Helen, Verdie Kay, and Joy; and to my uncle, Gary Walton."

While Dwight's dad owned a gas station in Columbus, his mom did some factory work and was also employed as a keypunch operator. They were a two-income family at a time when a stay-at-home mom was the middle-class norm, and with two other children following Dwight, the Yoakams needed those incomes to live comfortably, if not opulently.

There's a touch of humor in the title—where "Rightin'" suggests that those educated in Pike County never learned to "right" too well—but the lyric is dark, which would become so characteristic for Yoakam. If the shimmering fantasy of life in the North is a promise betrayed, the retreat from it is unthinkable. There's nothing to look forward to, and there's no looking back.

"Have you ever heard a mountain man cough his life away, from digging that black coal in those dark mines?" sings Dwight, his voice emotionally flat, laconic, with a tight-lipped stoicism that would become a musical trademark. "If you had, you might just understand the reason they left it all behind."

While there's an element of creative projection in much of the song, as in so much of Dwight's material, the third verse is pure memory, with the sweetness of familial redemption: "Have you ever seen 'em put the kids in the car after work on Friday night/Pull up in a holler about 2 a.m. and see a light still shinin' bright/Those mountain folks sat up that late just to hold those little grandkids in their arms/And I'm proud to say that I've been blessed and touched by their sweet hillbilly charm."

So there you have it. The promise of a better life up north is an illusion. Any nostalgia for a better life down south would be a lie. What's real is the character of the people forged by such tough circumstances, the warmth engendered by families who have only each other as respite from the cold, hard facts of life. And even if these words have been written and sung by a city kid, every last one of them rings true, the hillbilly legacy he claims for himself a birthright, as the grandson of a coal miner—his mother's father, Luther Tibbs—whose life would influence much of his music.

Pikeville without Columbus might not have produced the music of Dwight Yoakam; Columbus without Pikeville *never* would have. Except as the home of Ohio State—which vies with the University of Texas at Austin as the country's largest university, with both accommodating some fifty thousand students—Columbus lacks much in the way of urban identity, not to mention artistic imprint. Few know that in a state with more than its share of sizable cities—Dayton, Toledo, Akron, Canton, and so on—that Columbus is the largest, with a population of 770,000, greater than the populations of Cleveland and Cincinnati combined (if we disregard the surrounding metro areas). Yet those two are major league cities, where Columbus is Big Ten, state fair, state capital, where Wendy's was founded. It's almost smack dab in the middle of a state that is Rust Belt to the north, bluegrass to the south.

"Quick, what do you think about when you hear the words 'Columbus, Ohio'?" begins a *New York Times* story from July 30, 2010, on the city's indistinct image. "That's the problem that civic leaders here hope to solve." The article proceeds to mention various slogans the city has attempted to promote—"Discover Columbus" and "Surprise, It's Columbus," before the current "There's No Better Place"—and then concludes with a native's sardonic suggestion: "Columbus, We Are So Not Ohio." It also quotes the local head of tourism: "Columbus has not had a bad image. It has just had no image."

Little wonder, then, that when Dwight Yoakam established a strong image as an artist, first in Los Angeles and soon in the wider world of country music, it was stamped by a tiny hamlet of Kentucky, which he'd left as a toddler but returned to often, rather than by the largest city in Ohio, where he was raised and schooled, where he was a member of the school drama club and a drummer in the concert band.

"I had a real Rogers snare because I'd started playing in school, where you could be part of instrumental music," Yoakam remembers. "For me, it had to be either guitar or drums because that was the rock and roll world. Those were the only instruments I was interested in. And school didn't encourage guitar slinging. *No siree*! You could play that clarinet, but you don't see a whole lot of clarinet on *The Ed Sullivan Show* or *Hullabaloo*."

Dwight remembers himself in Ohio as someone who never quite fit. "In Columbus, believe me, they looked at me like I was a little odd," he says. "I was queer, in that sense. I was an odd bird." But what might have been considered odd was the part of Dwight that he didn't necessarily show at school. Some of it was the fundamentalist Christianity that the family had brought with them from Kentucky, their worship at the Church of Christ in Columbus where other Southern transplants congregated.

Music at the church was unadorned with instrumentation, and the purity of that music (as well as some of the melodic progressions) stayed with Dwight. He also mingled at church with plenty of students from Ohio State, even grad students, who shared his interest in music and could show him a trick or two on guitar, which he'd started trying to play while still in grade school. When he made his first tentative foray into Nashville after graduating from high school, connections from church provided him with what he calls a "safe landing."

Yet the musical influence of his religion started even earlier and ran deeper: "My family read the Bible constantly, and it gave me the ear for rhyming schemes," he explained. "The King James Version is musical. So I've got that from three or four years old, hearing that read aloud." (It also influenced his personal habits; even after he became the master of the drinking song and made his living in honky-tonks, he never touched a drop of alcohol, and never indulged in drugs.)

There was plenty of secular influence as well. His parents had a lot of country and western music around the house, much of it acquired from the Columbia Record Club, then ubiquitous with its offers of a dozen albums for a penny (with the commitment of buying a dozen more at list price with exorbitant shipping and handling charges, and if you didn't remember to return the card every month, you'd get records you had no interest in owning).

Johnny Horton's Greatest Hits was one of the most played (it was on Columbia, and the record club tended to favor releases on its own label). It was one that my family got from the Columbia Record Club as well, and which I remember playing to death, having no idea that Horton was considered to be in a different musical category than any of the other hits in power rotation on Top 40 radio. "North to Alaska," "Sink the Bismarck," and "The Battle of New Orleans" were hugely popular story songs, just like Marty Robbins's "El Paso," another AM hit that I never knew was considered country.

I paid less attention to the earlier stuff on the album, such as "Honky-Tonk Man," a breakthrough hit for Horton in 1956 that would become Yoakam's first signature tune, attracting fans that had never heard the original. The year it climbed the charts for Horton was the year that Yoakam was born.

Plenty of other music made a strong impression on him: "One of my earliest memories is my mother and aunt sitting on the sofa and singing at the phonograph player," he says. "We didn't sing *with* it. We sang *at* it. And the song was Hank Locklin's 'Send Me the Pillow You Dream On.' And just *bellerin'* it to the heavens!"

If music could make you feel the way you wouldn't otherwise, it could also help you say what you couldn't otherwise: "I was listening to everything on the radio. But I would listen alone to Stonewall Jackson albums that my parents had," he continues. "We had this one around the house that my dad bought as this anniversary present for my mom, with this song 'Don't Be Angry' as a love note to her. It was sweet. They broke up some years ago, but I still remember this as a comment on what music is to people in their lives. He was a rough, tough guy, but [the lyric] 'Don't be angry with me darling' let him say something to my mother that he was incapable of saying on his own."

So much more attention has been paid to the place Dwight comes from (or at least the place where his music has its strongest roots) than the times that shaped his life, but his experiences as a child of the 1950s and '60s left an artistic imprint every bit as strong as the geographical one. On Top 40 radio, you could hear Buck Owens as well as the Beatles, Stax/Volt records, and garage-band psychedelia. Those genres and more would find their way into Yoakam's own music—where the honky-tonk meets the garage band meets the countrypolitan polish—representing a natural outgrowth of his formative listening experiences.

Radio was a powerful influence on Yoakam and on practically every American music fan of his (and my) generation, but television made an impression that was every bit as strong, possibly even more so where his performing persona is concerned. He was born into the television era and came of age with the explosion of color. Television made the Monkees a more powerful—or at least more intimate—influence on Yoakam than the Beatles. The Beatles were just a little bit before his time, while the Monkees arrived when he was just the right age.

Let's let Dwight riff a little: "I was a Monkees kid. For a ten-year-old like myself, the Monkees were a cultural access point that the Beatles weren't. I was an oldest kid, teaching myself, and the Beatles were a little bit beyond my grasp. Television delivers the Monkees to me in a different way; *A Hard Day's Night* was not on TV in 1965. And I was not old enough at eight to take myself to the movies. I could see them on *The Ed Sullivan Show*, but that was too godlike. The Monkees, on the other hand, came inside my living room, and there was a familiarity that allowed me to really understand what this new thing was.

"I had the first two Monkees albums, and I couldn't have gotten a better education, retrospectively, in songwriting, when you think about it, than listening to Neil Diamond, Carole King, Boyce and Hart compositions. The world told in two-and-a-half to three minutes. And Mike Nesmith brought that Texan's aesthetic, and he was an accomplished songwriter. Country rock really owes a debt to Mike Nesmith for writing 'Different Drum,' the first hit by Linda Ronstadt when she was with the Stone Poneys. So listening to that at ten or eleven years old, with this half-baked set of drums, I'd literally play along.

"Mike later became a friend of mine, introduced to me by my dear friend Dennis Hopper," he continues. "Mike told me one time, he was out here on a motorcycle trip with his girlfriend in northern California, and he sees a guy with a bunch of kids and says, 'I think that's Mel Gibson.' And Mel looked around and said, 'I know you. *Oh my God, you're a Monkee.*' And that was, like, thirty years later."

So, by the standards of Columbus kids in the 1960s, Dwight's cultural experiences were pretty much in the mainstream. Maybe he heard a little more Stonewall Jackson at home than some of the others, and practiced a more fundamentalist religion than most, but he listened to the same radio, watched the same TV. And these experiences became as authentically his as his family's Kentucky legacy and their weekend drives south down Route 23.

Just look at Yoakam onstage or on video. Consider the way he wears his cowboy hat, twitches his leg, cradles and thrusts his guitar. He didn't get any of that from Kentucky. Or Ohio. Or even from the radio. He got it all from television, where gunslingers and guitar slingers all but merged in his mind into a single heroic image.

"I was influenced by every guitar slinger I ever saw on television," he agrees. "I was born in 1956, and TV kind of exploded in the late '50s, when it was firing on all eight cylinders. From *Cheyenne* to *Sugarfoot* to *Have Gun, Will Travel* to *The Rifleman*. And TV had moved to the West Coast and had almost become an exclusive province of Hollywood. TV moves from that theatrical-like soundstage to the film-like execution of serialized television.

"So my life, oddly, because of the medium of television, was profoundly impacted and influenced to always come [to Los Angeles]. By the look, the swagger, the explosion of the cowboy TV series, this gunslinger imagery that dovetails on any given weekend night with Ed Sullivan and any other guitar slinger performances. I have a picture from when I was eighteen months old with this big old guitar and trying to cock my leg to impersonate what I saw on TV."

When he made the big leap in high school from watching music to performing it, impersonation rather than self-expression was the impetus. Except for his drumming in the concert band, his major artistic pursuit was theater. He'd played Charlie in *Flowers for Algernon* and James in *The Miracle Worker* as a student at Northland High School in Columbus (class of '74).

He'd received musical encouragement from his theater teacher, and he'd hosted the school's variety show, where making music was like playing dress-up. In the wake of Sha Na Na, he had a '50s-style rockabilly band, Dwight and the Greasers, whose debut at school established the course his life would take. "That was what I'd been living to do," he remembers. "At sixteen, I realized I'd been waiting the first fifteen years of my life for this band, this moment, this stage. Three hundred and fifty non-related people and the place went a little berserk. *The girls did!* And I did become fascinated with what possibilities were there for me if I had the necessary guidance and focus."

The guidance and focus would require a move to the West Coast, but the drive was already there.

3

South of Cincinnati, West of Columbus

WHEN DWIGHT YOAKAM LAUNCHED his recording career and quickly won fans in both the country mainstream and the alternative fringes, his music sounded as if it had been forged in the coal mining country of Kentucky. But it was really in Southern California where Yoakam developed his signature style and found his destiny. He was a musical product of Los Angeles, defined by how different he was from all the other musical products of Los Angeles, which itself was another world from the assembly-line production of Nashville.

If this were a different sort of biography, one encompassing the minutiae of the life rather than focusing on the progression of the music, we'd have to devote a chapter or more to Nashville, where Dwight made his first stab at a musical career after a brief stint at Ohio State in his hometown of Columbus convinced him that higher education was not for him. His house had never been filled with books, though Dwight's inquisitive mind found kindred spirits among the grad students from the near South who attended their church, and his vague plans to pursue a degree in history or philosophy suggested some direction after his graduation from Northland High School in 1974. To what goal?

"Oh, man I had no idea," admits Yoakam, whose restless spirit led him to quickly abandon his studies. So he decided to seek musical fame and fortune in Nashville. Why Nashville? Because it was close, a short day's drive from Columbus, less than four hundred miles. (A pudgy, Indiana high school dropout named John Hiatt had decided to relocate to Nashville for pretty much the same reason. It seemed a whole lot easier and less extreme for a Midwest kid than trying to tackle New York or L.A.) Plus, Dwight had what he called a "landing spot" in Nashville—friends from his church had family there.

Otherwise, he had no more of a sense of destiny than most other high school grads that had given college a try before deciding that since they no longer *had* to go to school they didn't want to. Only in retrospect did the sojourn to Nashville become symbolic in the Dwight Yoakam mythos, some saying that he had somehow been spurned there so he had to find somewhere else where his music would receive its proper embrace.

Nashville didn't reject Yoakam. Nashville didn't even notice him. It offered him a job as an extra at Opryland, the theme park surrounding the suburban relocation of the Grand Ole Opry from the venerable Ryman Auditorium. (Opryland has since become a shopping mall, and, yes, there's a metaphor here.) He was an eighteen-year-old kid with no band, no connections, no songs—well, a few formative efforts, but Yoakam wouldn't really begin to mine the musical possibilities of Kentucky and establish a hillbilly persona to fit until his subsequent move two thousand miles west would give him greater perspective on what he'd left behind and what he could make from it.

Yoakam's music most certainly would have turned out differently if he'd found an enthusiastic reception in Nashville, with its recording industry more interested in polishing brand new urban cowboys than reincarnating the raw-edged, age-old music of the honky-tonk man. And his life could have turned out very differently had he remained at Ohio State, where he would have been one of the many who had once dabbled in music and theater but had left them behind in high school.

But neither Nashville nor Ohio State had panned out, so when a musician friend in Columbus with a car urged Dwight to accompany him on a cross-country joyride to Los Angeles in 1977, Yoakam didn't need a whole lot of convincing. After his brief anonymity in Nashville, he continued to play music in Ohio, singing the songs of Buddy Holly and the Everly Brothers, things that were closer in spirit to what would become neo-rockabilly than contemporary country.

Oddly enough, one of the hits that had convinced him that he had something special to offer was "Rock On" by David Essex, where the hitch in the voice of the Brit, almost a hiccup, was something akin to the choke you'd hear in the vocals of the Appalachian bluegrass Dwight had heard in Kentucky. What seemed exotic to the rock fans in Columbus sounded familiar to him.

Even greater validation came from the popular dominance of the roots-oriented Creedence Clearwater Revival, a band that bridged FM album acceptance and AM single hits and had become one of the most consistently successful commercial acts of the 1970s. Creedence gave Dwight some hope that he could do what they had done; mainstream country simply wasn't on his radar at the time. The hard-edged country music he'd loved was no longer in vogue in Nashville or on the airwaves. "Lookin' Out My Back Door" was a Creedence hit, and it was more country ("listenin' to Buck Owens") than country.

"I was really inspired by Creedence Clearwater Revival illustrating that country-hyphen-rock/pop could be pertinent for a young audience," explains Yoakam. "The Byrds were folk rock, but country rock is John Fogerty. 'Cause you can't get any harder rockin', and in some places more country, than Creedence—a real hybrid that was a commercial success."

But Creedence came from the Bay Area, a long way from the bayou country that so much of its music conjured. Whatever rootsy authenticity the band's music evoked was a geographical fantasy, an illusion—an art. And Dwight was heading for L.A., "swimming pools, movie stars," as the theme from *The Beverly Hillbillies* had put it. Despite the tinsel and glitz of a city where all of the cowboys were rhinestone ones—though Yoakam, of course, was no more of a cowboy than any of them—there was another beacon of inspiration that shone as brightly as Creedence.

"That first Emmylou Harris album is what drew me out here," he says of his move to L.A. "My junior and senior year in high school, I was in love with both Linda [Ronstadt] and Emmylou. And so, when my buddy said, 'Man, you've got to come to L.A.,' I said, 'Yeah, I know, Emmylou Harris is out there. There's a scene somewhere out there that I can tap into.'"

At least there had been. And maybe there would be, but it took another four years of scuffling—working here on a loading dock, there as a short-order cook—and playing the bars in the Valley before Dwight recorded his first demo tape and started to receive higher profile gigs at the venerable Palomino and the hipper Club Lingerie. And then it took *another* three years after that demo for Dwight to release *Guitars, Cadillacs, Etc., Etc.* as his debut EP, and it was a couple years after that when his 1986 major-label album of the same name was released, adding four cuts (including the title track) to the six songs previously issued on the EP.

So Dwight may have come out of nowhere, as far as the world of music was concerned, and country music in particular, but it had been almost ten years since he had graduated from high school, and he was on the cusp of thirty by the time he became an overnight sensation. In retrospect, such success appears preordained, but at the time it seemed anything but. His career path required the patience and perseverance of an artist who had more of the latter than the former.

His friend with the car who drove him out left a month later. Before moving to Hollywood, to an apartment in the Hills that friends remember as slightly larger than a closet, slightly smaller than a garage, he was working in nearby Long Beach. There he made his initial foray into show business—not in music but in theater, with a role in a local production of *Heaven Can Wait*.

Dave Alvin says he likely ran into Dwight when they were both employed as short-order cooks in Long Beach, though it would be a couple of years before their more significant encounter at the Palomino. By then, the lead guitarist and songwriter of the Blasters was in a position to help unknown artists who impressed him, introducing them to the band's roots-rocking fans with opening slots. Dwight would later repay the favor by recording Alvin's "Long White Cadillac," introducing the song's narrative of the last night of Hank Williams's life to country radio.

Given the seminal influence of Creedence on Yoakam's music, it's fitting that he would find musical kinship with Alvin, who mined a seam of what would subsequently become known as "Americana" for riches similar to that in the songs of John Fogerty. On the album release of *Guitars, Cadillacs*, Yoakam offered special thanks to Alvin and the Blasters, as part of a select few "who believed when nobody else cared."

"I later discovered that we'd both been cooks in Long Beach in the late '70s, worked half a mile away from each other," remembers Alvin with a laugh. "I was a cook in a Middle Eastern restaurant that was predominantly vegetarian. And Dwight was a cook at a place called Hamburger Henry's.

"I'd go there and get a burger after cooking vegetarian for eight hours. And Dwight didn't get famous *only* for doing drinking songs, but he did quite a few. So it's kind of ironic, this vegetarian cooking hamburgers, who had never had a hamburger in his life, and singing drinking songs, and he'd never had a drink. And singing them pretty persuasively."

The years between driving to Los Angeles in 1977 and cutting his first demo in 1981 were plainly productive ones for Yoakam in terms of writing. All of the ten songs that Yoakam would cut for that demo would subsequently be re-recorded for his first three albums, except for "Please Daddy," which he'd written in high school, once again using his imagination. It's a song sung from the perspective of a young daughter who is trying to console her father (and likely herself) that things will be all right after he and her mother had split up.

To listen to those revelatory demo recordings, first issued on the four-disc, 2002 retrospective *Reprise Please Baby: The Warner Bros. Years*, you'd never suspect that "Please Daddy" would be the only track he wouldn't re-record for release because it's as good as many of them. Others more directly reflected his own experience, as he explains of "You're the One," a highlight ballad of the demo but not included on a Yoakam album until his third. "I'd written that in 1978 about this girl I'd grown up with, a beautiful preacher's daughter who broke my heart," he remembers. "She went to the prom with me. Though, again, it goes well beyond the literal. I was a senior in high school, I was crushed, and I got over it."

Living in Southern California gave Yoakam a fresh perspective on what he'd left behind, offering even more of a contrast than he'd experienced between Columbus and Kentucky.

Raised in the former, he recognized that the latter provided the inspiration that would distinguish him from the run of the country-rock mill. Not necessarily his own experiences, or even those of his immediate family, but songs in which he could use that legacy for some imaginative reshaping. "Miner's Prayer" is two generations and a hundred miles from Yoakam's upbringing; "South of Cincinnati," a track from the *Guitars, Cadillacs* EP and LP that shows a short story's command of detail, uses the marriage of his grandparents, together more than fifty years, to explore the alternate reality of a loving couple separated by alcohol and pride.

One of the ironies of Yoakam's musical progression in California, when he began to write almost exclusively of Kentucky and cast himself as a pilgrim from the bluegrass backwoods, is that in urban Columbus he'd distinguished himself by his ability to channel the country-rock that had been emerging from Southern California. And that was the music he considered his strength when he made the move west.

"When I got out here, I would do 'Carmelita,' Linda Ronstadt's version," he said of the song he would later cover in a style closer to Warren Zevon's original. "I would do the Eagles. I was always country rock, because my voice, my family, was country. So at the moment that country rock was starting to inundate AM radio, I could play the Eagles, I could sing it. That was me."

Yet it was his writing that would allow Yoakam to discover who he really was, or at least develop a persona that would prove compelling to the indie, roots-rocking punk crowd even before he plunged into the country mainstream. Even his Li'l Abner-ish name seemed to exude authenticity, making him sound a little like the bumpkin he never was or would be. You couldn't capitalize on a name like that by continuing to sing Eagles covers.

"With writing, I controlled my own destiny," Dwight says. "'I'll Be Gone' made me realize I could do it in my own way. And 'It Won't Hurt' was written about the same time."

"It won't hurt when I fall down from this bar stool," sings Yoakam, strumming his acoustic guitar, as we sit in his office. "And it won't hurt when I stumble in the street. It won't hurt 'cause this whiskey eases misery, but even whiskey cannot ease your hurting me."

This was the second cut on the demo tape, following "This Drinkin' Will Kill Me." Another highlight from the demo that would wait until his third album for release, "I Sang Dixie," recounts the story of a man from the South who had died "on this damned old L.A. street," after "the bottle had robbed him of all his rebel pride."

In those early L.A. days, he was billing his band as Dwight Yoakam and Kentucky Bourbon. Yet, as Dwight would subsequently tell any interviewer who bothered to ask, he had never touched a drop of alcohol and likely never would. First, because his fundamentalist religion prohibited it. Second, he had seen what it could do, during years of playing at bars for drunks and in close relationships with those who suffered from the disease of alcoholism.

"I wasn't raised on it and had never witnessed alcoholism at close range until I knew a guy named Richard Christopher," says Dwight. "He was quite a piece of work, a Runyonesque character. He was six-foot-six, and he was originally from Cleveland, Ohio. He developed coupon books to sell to people. He had a master's degree from Ohio State and ended up being drafted into the Korean War.

"He was just this carny guy. I would listen to him tell these war stories. And he was also a severe alcoholic. But functional. He managed this apartment complex and was also wheeling and dealing with trading furniture, stuff like that. He walked with a cane and looked like Ichabod Crane. His drink of choice was vodka with prune juice or anything else. I'd stop by and listen to Dick Christopher ramble on a little bit. And I wrote 'It Won't Hurt' about him."

So, the teetotaler began to specialize in drinking songs, a venerable tradition of honky-tonk music, but one that had fallen from fashion in the sanitized country music of the late 1970s and early 1980s. The airwaves were no longer filled with the likes of neo-honky-tonker Gary Stewart, who lived the life of which he sang, and who had enjoyed considerable country success early in the 1970s with breakthrough hits including "Drinkin' Thing" and "She's Acting Single (I'm Drinkin' Doubles)." As country was starting to veer toward soft rock, there wasn't as much emphasis on hard liquor.

Yoakam's subject matter and sound distinguished him as a honky-tonk throwback, and he had no problem reconciling such material and the bars where he performed it with the religion in which he was raised.

"I didn't feel that my salvation or destiny was imperiled by that," he says. "But I'd also witnessed enough drinking and drugging in the early '70s, which led to the debauchery of the late '70s, Studio 54 and all that, where there couldn't have been a more depraved world to step into. I'd been playing this place called the Corral [where Yoakam and Kentucky Bourbon had become the house band] and watching people stumbling through it, getting through the rest of that night, and that's what that song is about. You don't have to live it to write it."

But if you were going to sing it, you had to be able to sell it, to convince listeners of your sincerity, your authenticity, of your ability to know and share what they were going through because you had been there too. A cynic might claim that Yoakam was to honky-tonk what the Monkees were to a rock band. But Yoakam recognized how much craft, spirit, and inspiration had gone into those Monkees' hits. And after decades of playing classic country records and years of playing bars, Yoakam knew how honky-tonk authenticity sounded. Even if the songs he wrote weren't literally true to his experience, he made them ring true. Where hillbilly music is concerned, Dwight's a believer.

4

Corvette Cowboy

DWIGHT YOAKAM DIDN'T HEAD WEST in order to plant the flag of country traditionalism and reclaim that musical territory as his own. He was smart enough to recognize that if he wanted a career as a mainstream country artist, country radio was crucial, and Nashville was the key. And that such success would likely come at a cost that a strong-willed artist, inspired by Creedence Clearwater, Emmylou Harris, Johnny Horton, and Stonewall Jackson, wouldn't be willing to pay. So he went west to become a country-rock star, to a city that encouraged transformation, reinvention.

"I knew my singing voice could marry with a style that was not so pure country," says Yoakam of his ability to channel the Eagles and his initial ambition to ride the next wave of country rock. "And I had the jeans, the boots . . . There was a whole *Hud* element to that cowboy culture that I knew that could be introduced, the Route 66 Americana, not the Nashville Dixie country. Beyond James Dean, beyond *Giant*. This Route 66 Corvette cowboy. So let's just call it that—it's beyond Cadillac Cowboy. It's Corvette Cowboy."

The jeans he had brought from Columbus, though Los Angeles is where he would learn to wear them so tight he seemed poured into them. The boots had come from Hollywood, from TV and movies, an image emblazoned on his retina since boyhood, decades before he'd headed west. The car . . . well, he had no car, but the Corvette was integral to the vision that he has since fulfilled. Today, he tools around L.A. in a sleek black 'vette, the latest in a series, with a teeth-rattling sound system.

Once he had a car (though not yet a 'vette), Los Angeles was where the Corvette Cowboy could drive free, unfettered by the conservative constrictions of Nashville. Los Angeles was home of the high-flying Eagles—the former backup band to Linda Ronstadt, the band that inherited the country-rock mantle from the Flying Burrito Brothers and would become a bigger success than anyone had ever anticipated for such music. They became so big that the Eagles and their ilk were widely disparaged among the roots-punk crowd that would soon become Yoakam's breakthrough constituency. Since the Burritos, and the deification of the late Gram Parsons, the whole "country-rock" tag itself had fallen into critical disrepute. It was "rock lite" (as the mainstream country that would draw so heavily from it a couple of decades later would be), lacking the edge or the muscle of the best rock. Or the best country, for that matter. It had diluted the strengths of those disparate strains for a watered-down fusion of cocaine cowboys, tequila sunrises, and singer-songwriter mawkishness.

If country rock was the goal when Yoakam headed for Los Angeles, it was largely a mirage by the time he was making music there. The Eagles themselves had flown their separate ways in acrimonious dispute, jettisoning original members who had stronger ties to the earliest incarnation of country

rock (former Burrito Bernie Leadon and Poco's Randy Meis-
ner) in favor of the harder rock of guitarist Joe Walsh and the
R&B influence of founder (and Detroit native) Glenn Frey.

The likes of Firefall (launched by former Burrito Rick Rob-
erts), the New Riders of the Purple Sage, and so many others
were long gone and not missed, memories of an era of buck-
skin fringe and muttonchop sideburns. Neil Young had em-
barked on a series of stylistic experiments, leaving the coun-
trier (and wimpier) Crosby, Stills, and Nash behind (though he
would rejoin them on and off). When Dwight arrived in L.A. in
1977, punk was establishing itself as a rebellion against soft-
er, flabbier rock, bloated by corporate and arena excess. But
commercial success—the sort to which Yoakam aspired—was
anathema to punk purity.

What punk shared with the music that Yoakam strived to
make was a belief that something essential had been lost to
sixteen-track studio overdubs, to larger-than-life arena ges-
tures, to the commodification of the multiplatinum music
industry. However you defined "real," authenticity had been
sacrificed to artifice. And the longer Dwight stayed in Los Angeles, the stronger his ties to Kentucky (and not Columbus)
seemed to him.

The rock of that era was largely rudderless, but country
music was even more without direction, still in its *Urban Cowboy* hangover, after the success of that 1980s movie that was
so much mechanical bull to country purists. It had yet to be
transformed by its savior (or Antichrist?), Garth Brooks, who
would recast pretty much everything about the music—from
its marketing to its stagecraft to its popular explosion— by
the beginning of the 1990s.

So Dwight was largely operating in a vacuum, post-Burritos
and pre-Garth, during the crucial years of his musical matu-
ration between his pilgrimage to Los Angeles—broke, unknown, but brimming with confidence, determination, and

vision—and his belated breakthrough as a mainstream country artist with hip rock credibility almost a full decade later.

In the music industry, a vacuum creates opportunity. Even though there was no place where Dwight Yoakam really fit, during that decade in which country rock had run its course and alternative country had yet to be labeled as such, he had plenty of company among other artists who recognized the common spirit between stripped-down rock and hardcore country, and between punk rock and roots rock.

Not long after Dwight had arrived in L.A., Texas neo-honky-tonker Joe Ely toured England and forged a bond of mutual appreciation with the Clash (whose *London Calling* masterwork would find some of its music steeped in what would later be called "Americana.") Willie Nelson, Jerry Jeff Walker, and Doug Sahm still held court over legions of cosmic cowboys based in Austin, confirming that Texas was a whole 'nother country with a decided twang to its rock.

In the Midwest, Chicago folkie John Prine joined forces with a rockabilly band and cut some tracks with Sam Phillips, founder of Sun Records. (Prine and Walker would subsequently prove influential as businessmen. They left their major labels and proved that by targeting their audience they could make more profit selling fifty thousand copies of an album by themselves than they could selling multiple times that for a major label.)

Out west, the emerging Paisley Underground revived some embers of country rock, with the Long Ryders (led by Gram Parsons acolyte Sid Griffin) and Green on Red (featuring future Alejandro Escovedo collaborator Chuck Prophet) attracting a post-punk following, some of it shared with bluesier bands such as the Blasters. And bands with country or blues roots had more in common with rockabilly revivalists such as the Stray Cats than any of them had with, say, Duran Duran.

Even in the hub of country music, a band called Jason and the Nashville Scorchers (who would subsequently be persuaded to drop the "Nashville" from their name to the eternal regret of front man Jason Ringenberg) drew a slam-dancing crowd by finding a common denominator for unbridled rock and roll and the rawest country—enough to convince some that Hank Williams had been the original punk rocker. By then, Lucinda Williams had also launched her recording career as a folk-blues revivalist (rather than the alt-country Americana queen that she would become). And there were others, here and there, throughout the country, without a category. The point is, there was a widespread recognition that rock had lost something—its urgency, its immediacy, its *roll*—that it could reclaim by connecting with its roots in country (and blues), and that there was vitality beyond Album Oriented Rock and contemporary categories.

Yet radio play of some sort was crucial to Dwight Yoakam's career vision. And rock radio, amid the proliferation of arena rockers and MTV haircut bands, no longer played anyone who sounded remotely like Dwight. The rock artists with whom Dwight had something in common had been (and would continue to be) relegated to the commercial fringes. Though country seemed like a tighter format, locked perennially into a Top 40 mode—still stressing hit singles rather than albums—it actually offered more opportunity for a troubadour with an independent streak through much of the 1980s.

Again, this was the era post–*Urban Cowboy* and pre-Garth, a brief window of opportunity when the country industry would be surprisingly open to new ideas, fresh sounds, and artists who didn't seem much like the country stars who had preceded them. From the mid through the late '80s, the husband-and-wife team of Rodney Crowell and Rosanne Cash were the reigning couple of this emerging country music, both with ties to tradition (he from Emmylou Harris's Hot Band, she as the daughter of Johnny), but with an album-oriented appeal to those who had outgrown what rock had become.

Mavericks such as Steve Earle and Lyle Lovett were initially targeted toward mainstream country in the mid-1980s, though rock-and-roll-influenced duos such as Foster and Lloyd and the O'Kanes enjoyed greater commercial airplay. Earle and Yoakam would provide provocative parallels and initially seem like rivals of a sort, each reclaiming the "hillbilly" tag that the smoother countrypolitan types of the last decade or two had done their best to bury. Yet Earle defended Nashville, where he had moved from his native San Antonio (following the path taken by fellow Texans Townes Van Zandt and Guy Clark), when Yoakam vocally decried it.

"We butted heads a little bit, which was turned into this feud by some people, but there was never any personal animosity between us," says Earle of his relationship with Yoakam. "What we had in common is that we used the term 'hillbilly,' which pissed George Jones off. He said one time, 'We spent all these years trying not to be called hillbillies, and Dwight Yoakam and Steve Earle fucked it up in one day.'"

Laughing, Earle continues, "We were definitely the same graduating class, but I think we disagreed about why we were doing what we were doing. He was trying to make country records, and I was operating under false pretenses. I was always a folk singer, but I'd had a rockabilly band, and I got a record deal, and then I got another record deal. But I was making a singer-songwriter record, and what Dwight did was based on honky-tonk music as a specific art form. What I was trying to do was sneak a singer-songwriter album in on Nashville, and dress it up as a honky-tonk record. And I'm unapologetic about that now. Whatever it takes!"

And then there was the matter of Nashville: Yoakam attacking it, Earle defending it. "He pushed my buttons that way, and I resented it," admits Earle, who later relocated from Nashville to New York. "Nowadays, I sort of wonder what I was defending, because I defended that town right up to the time I left. And I don't really anymore.

"But Dwight and I did a double bill years ago. We played first, and then he went onstage and said, 'Okay, you've heard from Nashville, and now we're gonna show you the real thing.' First thing out of his mouth! And, okay, I did write 'Dwight Yoakam eats sushi' on the wall of the dressing room of the Forum. And I love sushi! But, at the time, it just seemed like a good thing to say if you were fucking with a 'new traditionalist.' Or whatever we were supposed to be."

Yoakam's disdain for Nashville notwithstanding, a decade after his brief, tentative foray into Nashville, it appeared that country radio had its ears open wider to a surprising variety of singer-songwriters than the rock industry based in Los Angeles did. The rock artists who shared Dwight's rootsy, rebellious spirit were deemed noncommercial (and not very interested in becoming commercial). The country airwaves had room for a creative rebel, if only for a brief interval, before Garth would render what passed for commercial success in the country music of the '80s as chump change.

Remaining in Los Angeles distanced Yoakam from the Nashville industry he would need to advance his recording career through radio play, but it allowed him to develop as a live performer, to work the circuit, sharpen his chops, find his audience, forge his own path. Nashville remained an industry hub of recording studios and Music Row offices without much of a club circuit or any sort of nightlife. It was a city of churches, not honky-tonks.

Not until Dwight had been in Southern California for four long years, writing songs, honing his craft, putting his music to the test of the honky-tonk crowd, seeing what worked and what didn't, would he have the opportunity to enter a recording studio and cut the ten tracks that would not only lead to his national breakthrough but provide the blueprint for his first three albums, the ones that would establish his persona and make him a star.

He had come to Los Angeles with the jeans and the boots. Now he had the songs. Soon he would have the sound.

From Kentucky Bourbon to Babylonian Cowboys

DWIGHT YOAKAM SHOT OUT of nowhere to national promi-
nence in 1986—a supernova, so fresh, so exciting, so *new*. If
he hadn't existed, somebody might have been tempted to invent him. And, given the nature of the music business, others would quickly try to reinvent him, as every Nashville label
schemed to market its own hunky, honky-tonk throwback,
making music that seemed to exist in a pre-countrypolitan
time warp. Some enjoyed considerable commercial success
(Ricky Van Shelton), others didn't (Stacy Dean Campbell).

But before anyone could try to reinvent Yoakam, Dwight
had to invent himself. Rather than an artist out of nowhere,
adrift from time and place, he was very much an artist of his
formative years—a child of the '50s and '60s, of cowboys on TV
and in the movies, of the Monkees on the radio and Creedence
on the stereo—and of his pilgrimage, to Hollywood, where
a Midwestern kid with family roots in rural Kentucky could

fulfill his destiny. He only seemed like an "overnight sensation" to those who hadn't watched his artistry germinate in Los Angeles for almost a decade, until he was almost thirty. And, really, nobody had been monitoring Dwight that closely, until the demo he cut in 1981—his first recording session—paid such serendipitous dividends.

Even in the wake of Dwight's subsequent commercial success, when he opened the door for some artists (e.g., Marty Stuart) who proceeded to forge distinctive paths of their own, none of those others created the sort of bridge that Yoakam did. Nobody else who revived a retro sound on commercial country radio enjoyed anywhere near the critical respect and hip cachet that Yoakam would sustain among rock critics, roots rockers, alternative radicals, and audiences likely to embrace artists on the commercial fringes (perhaps *because* they were on the commercial fringes, wearing the lack of multiplatinum success as a merit badge of integrity).

Yoakam's breakthrough was something of a game changer. Yet, as documented in previous chapters, it was a long time coming, beginning with his aborted trip to Nashville after his 1974 graduation. Through his years of obscurity, working his way up from clubs in the San Fernando Valley and outskirts—like his stint fronting the house band at the Corral in Lakeview Terrace—he generated little press attention or cult buzz whatsoever.

Even after he started playing semi-regularly at the legendary Palomino—the closest thing to a traditional honky-tonk in the L.A. area—he was mainly an opening act with a day job. Located in the unfashionable remove of North Hollywood, the Palomino seemed a whole lot closer in spirit to Bakersfield, a hundred miles away. A blue-collar bar by day (when it opened at 6 a.m.), the club had been around since the early '50s, hosting the likes of Patsy Cline and Johnny Cash, offering a home away from home for the harder-edged sounds of Bakersfield's Buck Owens and Merle Haggard. It had been reclaimed by the early '70s generation of country rockers, with Linda Ronstadt, the Burritos, and Emmylou Harris all gracing its stage. By the time Dwight started playing there in the early '80s, country rock had become passé, and the scenesters had moved on.

The teetotaling artist christened his band Kentucky Bourbon, reinforcing his ties to the bluegrass state (which he had visited mainly on weekends), as well as his credentials as a one-hundred-proof honky-tonker. Not that Dwight pretended to be something he wasn't. From his earliest interviews he would talk about being raised in Ohio amid a conservative Christianity that prohibited alcohol. But drinking was integral to the honky-tonk ethos, just as integral as the cowboy hat and boots that had never been part of his wardrobe in Columbus. His audience was drinking, and Dwight was fine with that. And the more they drank, and the more he sang about drinking, the better they liked him.

Kentucky Bourbon was a bar band, assembled to support a singer whose pinched phrasing and strong sense of yearning had become more pronounced, more distinctive, the longer and farther away he was from home. Whether opening for the club's headliners or performing all night in smaller bars, Yoakam played a utilitarian role, drawing dancers to the floor like a jukebox, but not really building much of a fan base through the original material he sprinkled in.

"All through the *Urban Cowboy* craze, Yoakam slogged through country gigs in Southern California, enduring requests to play Kenny Rogers and Eddie Rabbitt when he was offering his own songs and those of Johnny Horton, Flatt & Scruggs, and Ray Price," wrote Paul Kingsbury in the *Journal of Country Music* ("The Old Sound of New Country," Vol. XI, No. 1). "Meanwhile, the hip kids of L.A. were following hardcore, nihilist punk bands. That audience seemed as far out of ear-shot as Yoakam's honky-tonk could get."

Caught between soft, commercial country and the harder place of rock, Yoakam may have generated little attention through the early '80s, but fellow musicians who hung around the Palomino were starting to know who he was and notice how good he was. There was no inkling at the time that his music would ever find favor with a rock crowd or that there was any future in beating the dead horse of country rock, but maybe Yoakam could show country music what it was missing.

Joe Ely had already been straddling that seam between rock and country, and his Texas roadhouse music was generating a lot of press attention. He remembers Yoakam playing the Palomino as his little-known opening act.

"He was kind of a shy little guy who played a great set," says Ely. "He had that Bakersfield thing that was really interesting, because the Texas guys were more attracted to the blues and Willie and Waylon. So I thought Dwight was completely unique, with different inspirations than we had. I was really intrigued by his songs, and how he'd taken the rockabilly thing and the Bakersfield thing and turned it into his own style."

Was Ely surprised when that unique style made Yoakam a huge mainstream country star? "I guess I was surprised and not surprised," he replies. "Because even in those early days, he had huge determination, and he wouldn't let anything get in his way. And that's the way he's always been.

Such success was still a few years down the road, when Dwight would get his first recording shot in 1981. Gordon Schyrock, an engineer at United Western Recordings, offered Yoakam free time for sessions that he would produce when he wasn't booked with paying customers. If those tapes led to a deal, then Schyrock would receive his reward and produce his label debut. According to the liner notes by Holly George-

Warren for the 2006 reissue of *Guitars, Cadillacs, Etc., Etc.*, Schyrock had become impressed with Dwight after filling in for Kentucky Bourbon's regular bassist at the Palomino, an enthusiasm he shared with local guitar hotshot Jerry McGee.

McGee was familiar to six-string aficionados as a latter-day member of the Ventures, the legendarily twangy instrumental combo, and had worked in the studio with artists ranging from Elvis Presley to Bobby Darin. In the '80s, the Ventures were enjoying something of a revival and were gigging regularly at the Palomino with McGee playing lead. But it's likely that Mc-Gee's credit that cut closest to Dwight's heart was his guitar intro to the Monkees' "Last Train to Clarksville."

While using Yoakam's Kentucky Bourbon drummer Stu Perry and bassist Robert Wilson, Schyrock recruited an all-star array of area session vets. Pianist Glen D Hardin (who had played with Elvis Presley), pedal steel guitarist JayDee Maness (who had played with Hardin in Emmylou Harris's Hot Band and with Yoakam's future mentor, Buck Owens, as a Buckaroo), and multi-instrumental prodigy David Mansfield (who had worked with T Bone Burnett in Bob Dylan's Rolling Thunder Revue and the Alpha Band that it spawned) joined McGee to provide Yoakam with the sort of backing he'd never previously received. The session may have been Yoakam's, but he was far less heralded than so many of the musicians in the studio with him.

The ten cuts they recorded first surfaced for public consumption on 2002's four-disc *Reprise Please Baby: The Warner Bros. Years*, the boxed-set compilation of hits, rarities, and previously unreleased recordings that served as Yoakam's swan song from the label. But it's the deluxe reissue of *Guitars, Cadillacs, Etc., Etc.*, released in 2006 to commemorate the twentieth anniversary of that full-length debut, that puts those first recordings in their proper context.

That two-disc set serves as a Rosetta stone for Yoakam's artistry, tracing his five-year progression from virtual unknown to hot new star, framing that 1986 release with the demos that led to it and a triumphant live performance at the Roxy in Hollywood, one of the trendiest rock clubs on the Sunset Strip.

That early demo shows just how much Dwight had going for him when nobody was paying attention, how he was already a compelling vocalist with full command of his delivery and a bunch of original songs so strong that they would highlight his first three albums. But they also show what was missing, the dynamics that would make him appealing to mainstream country and roots-rocking fans alike, and would turn him and the new band recruited after those sessions into a performing powerhouse.

"You can hear me really trying to figure *me* out," he explained to George-Warren in those deluxe edition liner notes. "In some ways, there's a reckless kind of innocence in those sessions that belie the more planned, later versions of the songs . . . I was twenty-four years old, and I went in there late at night after I'd get off my air-freight driving job.

"Gordon was from Tulsa and part of that eclectic musical mix of Leon Russell, J.J. Cale. Gordon allowed me to gain an introduction into the world of professional recording in a way that permitted me to be left to my own devices—for better or worse, at any given moment. I wasn't experienced enough to edit myself. Ultimately, it was a healthy approach for me personally."

In retrospect, knowing that those sessions failed to land him a deal, and comparing them with the subsequent recordings that would succeed, one finds the strengths of the singer and his songs diluted rather than enhanced by the support he received. Too many arrangements show musicians competing for space, sometimes as if they were racing each other. And there's a self-consciousness to some of the retro flourishes, as if the arrangements were evoking the cornball affectation of *Hee Haw* or *The Beverly Hillbillies*. You can hear all the promise of what Yoakam would become in those tapes, but you can also see why those sessions didn't take him there.

"Gordon was a proficient engineer, but those demos didn't have the technical architecture," explains Yoakam. "Architecture" is a term that Dwight and others who worked with him frequently employ when discussing the progression of his recording career, one that suggests a crucial distinction. Dwight was already the artist—the guy with the voice, the songs, the nascent charisma. But he desperately needed a partner who could fulfill the role of sonic architect, who could lay the foundation, frame and scaffold the musical structure, supply what was necessary to give the songs the spare, sturdy support they required.

As detailed by George-Warren in the deluxe edition notes, that demo was targeted specifically toward Nashville, and that's where it was shopped, because there appeared to be no way that an artist who had come to Los Angeles with country-rock aspirations would find an audience in the rock world with his honky-tonk twang and pinched, nasal tenor.

She writes, "It's hard to believe that such an impressive batch of songs performed by, as Dwight calls them, 'exceptionally gifted musicians,' fell on deaf ears in Music City. But that's exactly what happened in 1982. The closest Yoakam came to a deal while shopping the tape in Nashville was the slight interest shown by one label exec to get Hank Williams Jr. to record 'I Sang Dixie.' 'Lucky for me that things didn't fall into place at the time,' Yoakam says today with a laugh."

Lucky because the song would become a signature chart topper for Yoakam himself, his biggest hit of his early career, though it would take until 1988 (and his third album) to do so. Lucky because the future held something brighter for Dwight than settling for songwriting credits on other artists' albums.

Lucky because the demo's failure led another struggling Los Angeles transplant to recognize exactly what those tapes were missing.

Pete Anderson later explained that he'd been interested in hearing the tape because of Jerry McGee. Nine years Yoakam's senior, the guitarist had come to Los Angeles as a rhythm and blues acolyte rather than a country fan, but Detroit had long been a mecca for Southerners looking for work in its auto plants and remained perhaps the strongest Rust Belt market for hardcore, gutbucket country (as immortalized in Bobby Bare's classic "Detroit City").

In the liner notes to the *Reprise Please Baby* anthology—also by Holly George-Warren—Anderson jokes that he'd been intrigued by the tape because of McGee's imprint: "I was always looking to steal [guitar] licks." He heard a role for himself as guitarist and producer, a place where the twang of a Telecaster—which had once played such a prominent role in hardcore country and the Bakersfield sound in particular, but had all but disappeared from the contemporary country airwaves—could reassert itself.

"So, Pete Anderson shows up, this kid from Detroit, and he was in some ways a mentor, an older brother, to me," says Dwight. "I met Pete after I'd done the demos, and he said, 'I'm a producer.' Pete was very cerebral. His father was a western Kentucky hillbilly transplant to the factories of Detroit [*DEE-troit*], and Pete was a little older than me.

"And we were able to put what had been a dreamlike vision for me for the past six years into a functioning unit. We became friends, and he said, 'I think what you're doing is conducive to what I do on guitar. You leave opportunities for that Haggard, James Burton, Buck-esque, Don Rich style of guitar.' 'Cause on the records a lot of time it's Buck playing his own leads.

"And I said, 'If you're game to try, let's try it.'

"Pete just said, 'I think it's a guitar-playing opportunity.' And I said, 'I think so too. You're the expert on that, I'm not. I think it could be something different from what the demos were.'

"And he said, 'I have a vision for it. Will you let me try to produce?'"

To fulfill his vision, the guitarist became Dwight's bandleader, recruiting highly regarded bassist J.D. Foster and fiddler Brantley Kearns, with drummer Jeff Donavan providing the sort of percussive wallop never heard in the music of Kentucky and rarely in Nashville. Yoakam dropped the Kentucky Bourbon tag and the band adopted a flashier moniker: the Babylonian Cowboys.

"Being the guitar knucklehead that I was, I didn't care much about hearing the songs, but I wanted to hear it because Jerry McGee played on it," says Anderson of his initial interest in Yoakam's tape. "So I went into the demo seeing if I could figure out what Jerry was doing that was cool. And in the process, I heard the songs. I'd been around songwriting and arranging and done demos with guys. So I was becoming something of a song doctor. Plus I grew up in Michigan, where I was bombarded by Motown and what a hit song sounded like at a very early age. I had kind of an ear for it.

"So when I listened to the songs, I realized they were really good," continues Pete. "They were bluegrass country. And it was almost like finding a guy who was writing songs as classic as Motown—*Nobody's doing this! Who wrote these songs?* It was shocking that they were so traditional sounding.

"He'd had a falling out with Jerry McGee, and I started playing with him," Anderson remembers. "We were a four-piece, and I got control of the intros, the outros, and the solos. So I could kind of box them in. In retrospect, going back and listening to the demo tape, basically the stuff just wasn't tightly arranged. The hook licks were random. The guy had gotten some really good players, but nobody really produced it. So there was this young guy who was driving the force with an acoustic guitar, and then these guys would pick up around him. They just bashed through it. So I really got control of the songs as an arranger on the bandstand and started to turn them around."

The focus provided by bandleader Anderson took Dwight's career path on the most unlikely detour in the annals of mainstream country. Or punk rock, for that matter. A few years before Nashville would hear any commercial potential in Yoakam's music, the streamlined urgency of the Babylonian Cowboys would receive a boisterously receptive embrace from a club scene that had forged a common bond between roots rock and punk rock, and was ready to welcome hardcore country into that circle as well. Other Los Angeles acts were flirting with incorporating country elements into a sound aimed at rock fans (with Lone Justice featuring Maria McKee the most highly touted at the time), but Yoakam was country incarnate.

He was the real deal.

Who You Callin' Cowpunk?

DAVE ALVIN HAS TOLD THIS STORY many times before, and it seems to get better every time. Dave's a natural storyteller. It's a talent he first flashed when he was lead guitarist and songwriter for the Blasters, the kings of the Los Angeles roots-rock scene of the 1980s, and has continued to demonstrate through his solo career as a troubadour, one whose finely detailed narratives draw from country, blues, folk, and rock alike.

After Gordon Schyrock and Pete Anderson, Alvin was the third major figure in short succession that would have a profound impact on Yoakam's career trajectory. And, in some ways, he was the least likely, for the Blasters, with the raw intensity their bluesy revivalism, drew mainly a punk rock crowd. And the only hint of country this crowd seemed to embrace was an emerging L.A. hybrid called "cowpunk," which was frequently as sloppy, anti-slick, and anti-commercial as the punk rock from which it had morphed. (Most of the early cowpunks had been in blitzkrieg bands before embracing the twang.)

Dwight wasn't sloppy. Dwight wasn't cowpunk. And Dwight wasn't in league with any subculture that had a profound disdain for selling records and having radio hits. Yet Alvin heard something *real* in Dwight, something undeniable, and the Blasters adopted Dwight as their opening act, giving him the opportunity to make their crowd his crowd. Since Yoakam had no other crowd, beyond the fellow musicians who recognized his talent, some of whom had been involved with the failed bid to win Nashville's ear, he wasn't about to be picky.

So let's listen to Dave tell the story of how he met Dwight Yoakam (again): "The first night I ever saw Dwight perform, my fiancée at the time and I had broken up, so I went into the Palomino to get drunk. There were maybe thirty people there, including the band, and I just sat at the bar and watched this guy deliver a totally complete, professional show, as if there were a thousand people. And it was *the band*—Brantley, Pete Anderson, J.D. Foster, Jeff Donavan—and they sounded like they would three years later when he was a star. Exactly the same show, pretty much.

"And I was floored. After their first set, I went backstage. I'd wallowed in my misery enough, [and] I'm normally pretty shy, but I didn't feel any qualms. I just walked up to Dwight and said, 'Order the limousine now! You're gonna be a star.' And so that kind of kicked off our friendship."

What's most significant about the story is that Alvin didn't simply believe that Yoakam was destined to become a star, but that he would become a *big country star*. When rock and country elements had previously commingled, the music had mainly won more favor with rock audiences than with the country crowd. Country was like a whole other country—with its own radio stations, dance halls, fan press, and audience base. You practically needed a passport to go there.

And Alvin didn't have one, though he plainly loved the country music from a decade or two earlier and found a common spirit between that and the blues base of the Blasters. For him to think an artist the Blasters would soon adopt as their opening act—introducing him to roots and punk audiences, where his music was embraced more enthusiastically than it might have been without the band's seal of approval—would be able to make the leap from the L.A. rock scene to the top of the national country charts was a remarkable act of prophecy.

"It seemed obvious," he says. "Yeah, totally. I was actually more of a fan of mainstream country then than I am now, or at least an observer. And country music, like pop music or anything else, has periods where they don't know what's going on. They figure it out, and then they don't know what's going on again. And then they figure it out, and then they don't know . . . You know what I mean? So when Dwight came along, the *Urban Cowboy* thing was dying, and it was being replaced by some pretty limp-wristed, lackluster stuff. The powers that be in Nashville just did not know what the next thing was: 'What's the next hat style?'

"I don't know if Dwight sat down and did demographic research, but I know that he was smart in that he knew that presentation was half of the ball game—the presentation of his image and to some extent that of the band," he continues. "And harkening back to the early-to-mid 1960s, visually. It wasn't like, 'Oh, I just found this shirt, and I think I'm gonna wear it tonight.' It was calculated. And that's not a bad thing. So, yeah, I knew he was gonna become a mainstream star."

And Alvin wasn't the only one. Bill Bentley, who would become a senior publicist at Warner Bros. while Dwight was at the label, was then working at the indie label Slash, home to the Blasters and X. He was also occasionally booking shows at the trendy Club Lingerie and writing about music for *L.A. Weekly* and other publications. He had been a writer, editor, and drummer in his native Texas, and the first time he heard Dwight at the Palomino, he was floored.

"Dwight was living in a garage, seriously, in the Hollywood Hills," remembers Bentley. "I think it had a bathroom and a door. And Bill Campbell, this great Texas guitar player that lived in L.A., said, 'There's a guy that you should meet who lives by you. His name's Dwight Yoakam, and he's really good.' And Campbell never says that about anybody.

"So one day Dwight just appears, and he gave me these two tickets and said, 'Bill Campbell said you might like to come and see me.' He'd been playing way out in the valley, and he was opening a show at the Palomino. The Palomino was *the* country club in L.A. going back to the 1950s, and I'd seen a lot of people there. And this guy gets up there, and I swear to God—I didn't get to see Elvis when he was young, obviously—but it was like, holy shit, how can this person be so good?

"Because at that time country music at its best was maybe John Anderson," he continues. "I think Kenny Rogers had taken over. It just really sucked. The Outlaws [Waylon, Willie, et al.] had kinda worn out their welcome, and they had never meant that much in L.A, anyway. In the four years that I'd been out there, I hadn't seen much country music that I'd liked.

"And then this guy—*goddamn*. Not only did he sound good, and the band sounded good, but he *looked* good. Dwight always looked impeccable, dressed to the nines in those short jackets and just the right cowboy hat. It was just the total package, and I knew this guy was gonna be huge. He had everything—the songs, the voice, the band, the look. And that was at the Palomino! Maybe about ten times in my life I've seen a band where I thought there's no way for this to miss."

You knew he would make it as a big country star? "Yeah, I did," he replies. "Remember, I was around for Rank and File and all the cowpunk movement. And from a million miles away you could tell that Dwight wasn't part of that. He played those shows with them and the Blasters and got in with that crowd pretty good. But it was apples and oranges."

Yet, somehow, an artist playing a traditional style of music that is commonly considered culturally conservative forged a bond with fans at the radical fringe of L.A. rock. And since he'd migrated to Los Angeles with country rock as his aspiration and made music steeped in country tradition for the rock crowd—just like Gram Parsons and John Fogerty had—he didn't consider his earliest embrace by rock fans to be all that unusual.

If there was a problem with this roots-punk genre, it was that it wasn't considered commercial. The fans loved the music *because* it wasn't commercial, seeing its lack of airplay and sales as a sign of artistic integrity. The music Yoakam had loved—country and rock alike—had always been popular, and the musicians that created it had always aspired to be commercially successful. So did Dwight, though it might have been hard to determine at that time how an artist could use Club Lingerie in Los Angeles as a launching pad to soar to the top of the Nashville music stratosphere.

Of the qualities his music shared with punk, Dwight remembers, "The spirit of what we were doing, the energy, the intent, was where the affinity was. That's what they got at Club Lingerie. The intention of our delivery, how profoundly we were connected to what punk had been. By that time, it had become cowpunk. The Dils had become Rank and File. But they weren't as proficient as the band that we had put together. And there was Sid Griffin's band, the Long Ryders. Our strengths and weaknesses were individual, but our intent was in common."

There was also a political dimension to what Dwight was doing, a reclamation of traditional country as the populist voice of the working class, the sound of a hardscrabble South (and of those who had moved north from there to urban factories) rather than the smoother sound of the suburbia that turned "hat acts" into chart toppers. ("All hat, no cattle," as they'd say in Texas.)

Dwight knew that country music had developed a bad reputation among the rock generation—*his* generation—and that even the '70s surge of country rock hadn't redeemed the genre. That music had been aimed primarily, if not exclusively, at rock fans, at those who weren't otherwise likely to turn the radio dial from FM album rock to the AM country station. Among rock fans, mainstream country had an image problem, one rooted in the politics of geography and class. In what would soon become known as "culture wars," country was on the wrong side.

"Country music in the sixties developed such a negative connotation with the youth of this country, and it was associated in kind of a cultural sense with the extreme right," Yoakam told Paul Kingsbury in 1985 (in an interview that has since been archived in the Country Music Foundation Oral History Project).

"I think there was such a stratification of the youth and the older generation that there was a period, a whole generation, where we did not pass the baton, so to speak, from one to the next, in terms of honky-tonk music, especially. It's extremely important that honky-tonk music have youth involved in it, because you remember that Hank Williams Sr. was a young man. I mean, he died at twenty-nine. So when he was twenty-four, twenty-five, twenty-six, twenty-seven, twenty-eight is when he was making the big waves that he was making. I think that's critically important."

Yoakam conducted that interview the week before his twenty-ninth birthday, so he knew of what he spoke. Between conservative politics and commercial polish, country music had lost its connection to the hillbilly exuberance of its youth, a spirit that Yoakam found more prevalent in the rock clubs of Los Angeles than the recording studios of Nashville.

Hank Williams was no cowpunk. But in his reckless abandon—the way he lived, the way he died, the music he made, the compromises he refused to make—he became the exemplar for every former punk rocker who began traveling that lost highway.

7

Honky-Tonk Man

LET'S RETURN TO THAT deluxe edition of *Guitars, Cadillacs, Etc., Etc.* to explain why we've dubbed it the Rosetta stone of Yoakam's musical development and subsequent career. The first disc opens with those 1981 demos produced by Gordon Schyrock, the ten Yoakam originals from his first recording session. The disc concludes with the ten cuts that constituted his major label debut, not issued until March 1986, the album that turned Yoakam into an overnight success and built a bridge between alternative rock and mainstream country that no other artist has crossed so successfully. Though many fall into the "too rock for country, too country for rock" chasm, none have enjoyed a fraction of Yoakam's commercial success, which he achieved without compromising his critical credibility.

Only four of those ten songs from the 1981 demo made the cut for the debut album, though others were plainly just as good and would see release and find great commercial success on Yoakam's follow-up albums. (And there's still that one song from those early demos, a divorce weeper titled "Please Daddy," that's as memorable as anything from Yoakam's early songbook.)

For better and worse, things had not proceeded according to plan after that 1981 demo. The plan had been to take the tapes to Nashville, where Yoakam's songs, singing, and seductive stage presence could be polished into a commercially successful product.

Though Nashville had proved barely interested in the songs, let alone the artist, the sessions nonetheless changed the trajectory of Yoakam's music and career. By catching the attention of Pete Anderson, Yoakam found the sonic architect who could frame his voice, provide an instrumental foil with a stinging guitar, and streamline his arrangements to best advantage. It's mainly hindsight that makes those 1981 arrangements sound busy, as if the guitars and fiddles were chasing each other's tails, but what Anderson added was clearly crucial, making the sound as important as the songs.

"Dwight's a brilliant lyricist, with a great voice as a gift from God," says Anderson. "And a gift for composition. He didn't struggle to write. He played me stuff he had written when he was very young, ten or eleven years old, and it was very poetic. So those two things were a powerful combination for him. It was just a question of what kind of music he was going to do. And he was learning to entertain and be comfortable onstage, but he had the confidence of knowing he had a really good voice from an early age.

"And I had arranging skills," Pete continues. "If he was like the agent, I was the manager. If he was the singer, I was the guitar player. If he was the songwriter, I was the arranger. If he was the artist, I was the producer. And at that time, he didn't want to do any of the things I wanted to do, and I didn't want to do any of the things that he wanted to do, which made it noncompetitive. I mean, I'd written a few songs, but I knew from hearing his songs that I'm not a songwriter like that. So I was smart enough to know I'd never go, 'Hey, man, let's do some of my songs.' And he was smart enough to know that he didn't understand arranging and he didn't want to play lead guitar. So we were uniquely two pieces of a puzzle."

What Anderson added to the mix extended beyond sound. Since he'd been around the L.A. scene longer than Dwight, he had some experience with the industry that Yoakam lacked. Not much, but just enough.

"I'm about nine years older than Dwight and had been playing on the scene a little longer, with a little more overall savvy of the business," he says. "But, believe me, both of us were very, very green in the business, even though I had a little more experience than he did. I remember going off with him to eat one night and explaining to him what publishing was. 'Cause he was working with a guy who said, 'Hey, man, if I take you into the studio late at night, can I have all your publishing?' And, he'd said okay. And I said, 'You did *what*?!' 'Cause I wasn't really sure what it was, but all my friends go, 'Never sell your publishing.' I had a friend who had a friend whose wife worked at Warner Bros.—you know, you're in the fringe of it in L.A., everybody's in the entertainment business in one aspect or another. So I'd heard certain things were important. And even though I was in my thirties and Dwight was in his twenties, we were really young. We were playing bars for thirty to forty bucks. And the top of that was, 'Can we get fifty bucks?'"

Perhaps even more crucial than career advice was the confidence Anderson had in Yoakam, a confidence that reinforced the artist's own: "One person can have a dream," says Pete. "And depending on your age and when you have it, people can beat it out of you. Peer pressure. But two people with a dream, that's a lot tougher. Because you've got somebody to turn to and say [of the doubters], 'He's nuts.' You become like a little mini gang. Instead of saying, 'Maybe they're right. Maybe I should go back to school. Maybe my hair is too long.' Whatever.

"Because I was a little older and a good guitar player on the scene, he had that respect for me. And I gave him all the support that he needed. I was being honest, bringing up little things, but basically I was saying, 'Hey, buddy, these songs are great. Don't let anybody tell you differently.'"

Would those songs and their singer have found an audience without Anderson? Hard to tell. They deserved to, but so do the songs of a lot of unheralded writers. If the pre-Anderson demo is any indication, they almost certainly wouldn't have found the roots-rocking, punk-rocking audience that gave Yoakam's music its first popular base, a base that would generate considerable press attention (where there had been none before) and would provide a launching pad for his unlikely ascent into mainstream country stardom.

Whatever polish Pete provided, his guitar gave Yoakam's songs more raw intensity than anything on those 1981 sessions. Pete was an unrepentant bluesman rather than a country session player, and his guitar served to unbridle Yoakam's musical spirit, giving it an edgy, dangerous quality that the punk crowd embraced as kindred. The rawer he sounded, the purer he sounded, and the purer he sounded, the more he appealed to a crowd that championed authenticity while rejecting the polish of commercial compromise.

What Anderson subtracted was as essential as what he added. There was now a primal purity to the interplay, where the demos had all sorts of very good musicians getting entangled with each other. Despite the augmentation of a few supporting musicians on the recording sessions that would produce Dwight's debut—including pianist Glen D Hardin, steel guitarist JayDee Maness, and multi-instrumentalist David Mansfield from the demo sessions—the basic band was a four-piece with each member making indelible, crucial contributions.

Anchoring the arrangements was the killer rhythm section of bassist J.D. Foster (whose MVP career would also include stints with the Silos, Lucinda Williams, the True Believers—with Alejandro Escovedo and Jon Dee Graham—and other critically acclaimed acts) and powerhouse drummer Jeff Donavan.

In the notes to his four-disc *Reprise Please Baby* box set, Yoakam explained his musical dynamic like this: "You combine drummers with mountain people, and you've got hillbilly music. That's what we're doing: Bill Monroe with drums." Of course, in geographical terms, what Yoakam was doing—or would soon be—had a whole lot more to do with hardscrabble Bakersfield than mountain-music Kentucky (where he'd often visited but barely lived). And one of the defining characteristics of Bill Monroe's music is that it would never have been able to accommodate any drummer, let alone one who played as fiercely as Donavan.

"Boy, he was a swingin' drummer," agrees Yoakam, himself a drummer back in his high school days and one who recognized the importance of percussion. "And had that great rim shot."

The front line teamed the guitars of producer Anderson— sometimes twang, sometimes scorch—with fiddler Brantley Kearns, the most recent addition to the band. And it is here that Anderson's production distinguishes itself from Schyrock's demos. The most striking example is the chiming riff that opens the love-'em-and-leave-'em tune "I'll Be Gone." What sounds like hokum, fiddle-driven overkill on the demos becomes a subliminal hook on the released version. Throughout the sessions, the spotlight focuses plenty on Kearns's fiddle, but he never sounds as if he is competing with or racing against the other instruments. From the handclaps to the backbeat, this is a band that plays like a band—whipcrack tight.

"He had twenty-one songs of his own when I met him, and the rest were Bill Monroe, Merle, old country stuff, and old bluegrass stuff that we kinda revved up," says Anderson. "And as we played them, I got a grip on them, but it wasn't until we decided to record them where we really defined them, arranged them, boxed them in. 'Cause we still had been jamming off the bandstand. So we started working from that perspective, and got Brantley Kearns, so we had fiddle and guitar, bass, drums, and acoustic. And we figured out what the head was and who played what solos and how long the solos were and how did we get from verses to choruses and things of that nature."

So they approached the recording project as something different from just capturing the band's onstage sound in the studio? "Oh, absolutely," responds Anderson. "Yeah, making it cohesive in terms of intros, outros, and solos, that was done on that record, every song."

Guitars, Cadillacs, Etc., Etc. had two separate iterations. The six-track 12" version released in 1984 had limited distribution through the tiny independent label Oak Records and a pressing reportedly of five thousand. Like a lot of press people, and as a fan of punk and roots rock, I tracked down the EP primarily because of Yoakam's association with the Blasters, whose pianist Gene Taylor guested on "Ring of Fire," the lone cover on what was otherwise a showcase of Yoakam originals.

My initial impression was positive—I loved the stripped-down sound and the stoic, reedy plaintiveness of Yoakam's voice—but the artistry seemed something of a throwback curiosity, particularly coming from L.A. To my ears, the music lacked the supercharged Texas twang of the Joe Ely Band or the punk urgency of Jason and the Nashville Scorchers (who would drop their own incendiary cover of "Ring of Fire" from their repertoire along with the "Nashville" from their name). It would take my first exposure to Yoakam live—a dynamic documented on the deluxe edition's second disc, the one that makes the set essential—to turn me from a fan into a raving apostle.

Other than "Ring of Fire," the only cut not previously de-moed by Schyrock was the beautiful, bittersweet balladry of "South of Cincinnati," an acoustic change of pace that puts an interesting twist on the songwriter's dual heritage in urban Ohio and rural Kentucky. It's a border song, one that evokes the palpable change that occurs below the Mason-Dixon line, "south of Cincinnati, down where the dogwood trees grow."

He sings the chorus from the perspective of a young woman whose boyfriend had left her to go north some fourteen years ago. She's been waiting, perhaps without hope, for his return ever since. Even if he'd asked, she wouldn't join him up there. For her, Kentucky is home. But if he ever decides to come back to his roots, she'll be there for him. Biographically, Yoakam is the guy who left, but the conviction he brings to the senti-ments of the song suggests that he knows Ohio can never be home in the way that Kentucky was.

The release of the EP spread the word on Dwight beyond the hipster circles of Los Angeles, with Jack Hurst of the *Chi-cago Tribune*, a critic who generally covered country from a mainstream perspective, syndicating a particularly influential rave. So it was time for Yoakam to take his show nationwide for the first time, but since he'd yet to find any support sys-tem (or safety net) in the country circuit, he depended on his roots-rocking benefactors, the Blasters.

"We'd done that previously with Rank and File and [Los] Lobos, so it was like, 'Okay, here's another guy we like that we can help,'" remembers Dave Alvin. "We got him a couple of California gigs, but the really big one was [when] we put him on a bunch of national dates that went from Texas all the way to the Ritz in New York City. When Dwight and the band opened up at the Ritz, there was a large Warner contingent there, and that was the first time the East Coast contingent of Warner people saw him. And within a month he was on the label."

In a 1985 interview with Yoakam, the *Chicago Tribune*'s Hurst writes, "Except for a rockabilly rearrangement of Johnny Cash's 'Ring of Fire,' the six cuts are as country as country's Top 10 was in the late 1950s and early 1960s: wailing fiddles, howling steel guitars, and a nasal enunciation and utter intensity that bring to mind the late Johnny Horton, early Merle Haggard, or the eternal Lefty Frizzell. The music of such people was great, as connoisseurs and long memories will affirm. But a modern reincarnation of it wowing young audiences of punkish bands with names such as Rank and File, Lone Justice, Blood on the Saddle, the Blasters, and Nick Lowe and His Cowboy Outfit?"

That such early praise should come from a mainstream country critic reinforced Yoakam's potential, which would ultimately be realized in sales of more millions than some of these other acts would ever sell in thousands. (Blood on the Saddle?) If the punk following made Yoakam a newsworthy novelty, commercial country was where his future would lie, though his music would retain an uncompromising spirit more common to punk and resist the formula of the Nashville assembly line—the sound that dominated country radio and had driven it into a rut.

While he was by no means alone in this, Yoakam saw country's future in reviving its past. Whether Hurst was prescient or had been tipped, the key to that commercial country breakthrough would come from the songbook of Johnny Horton.

"Honky-Tonk Man" was the kickoff track to the major-label release of *Guitars, Cadillacs, Etc., Etc.*, the first single, and Dwight Yoakam's first signature tune. The song would spend six months on the country charts, falling just short of the top (it reached number three, a career launch).

It was one of only four tracks added to expand the EP into an LP, which was otherwise reissued in close to identical packaging and gave Dwight the distinction of being one of the few artists whose major-label debut carried the note that it contained previously released material.

Anderson and Yoakam returned to the demo for another song, "Bury Me," teaming him with Maria McKee of the highly touted Lone Justice, a country-tinged band aimed at the rock market, where it would generate tons of publicity (mainly because of McKee's looks and voice) but never come close to enjoying the success that Yoakam did.

"Maria McKee was definitely a critics' darling and everybody wrote about Lone Justice," says Anderson. "Dwight kinda got into booking agent mode, where he'd call places and bend their ear until they'd say, 'Okay, come in and play.' We'd slip in under the more popular bands. So Dwight got us on a bill opening for Lone Justice at the Palomino, and the place was packed, and we started to get noticed by writers. So that's how we'd gotten on the radar."

Closing the ten-cut version was a fairly straightforward rendition of the Harlan Howard chestnut, "Heartaches by the Number." The remaining cut new to the LP was the title track, one that drew the line in the sand of the contention that would define Yoakam's relationship with country orthodoxy.

There had been no title song to the EP, but Yoakam provided one for the LP, with "Guitars, Cadillacs" filling in "and Hillbilly Music" in the place of the "Etc., Etc." Nashville blanched. The "hillbilly" tag was something that country had made a concerted effort to ditch, from the countrypolitan sophisti-cation of Chet Atkins and Billy Sherrill productions through the slick suburbanization of *Urban Cowboy*. And here was this punk upstart, tracking manure all over the split-level home that country had built for itself, reminding listeners of the music's outhouse era.

"They asked Pete if he could get me to change it, take the 'hillbilly' out," says Yoakam. "And Pete knew better. He said, 'No way.'"

Proudly emphasizing the hillbilly and the honky-tonk, Yoa-kam was prepared to launch himself after a decade of scuffling in Los Angeles. The question was whether the country—coun-try music, in particular—was ready for Dwight. Sharing fans with the Blasters and Los Lobos made Yoakam an interesting phenomenon in the Los Angeles club circuit, but such associa-tions were more likely to be a liability than an asset in main-stream country. For Dwight, the edge and energy he could bring to country music were not merely positives, they were crucial.

"The country music industry, in Yoakam's opinion, has ignored the obvious: namely that music appeals to a young audience (that is, the audience that buys records), when it's made by reckless, young artists," wrote Paul Kingsbury before the album's national release in the Nashville-based, histori-cally minded *Journal of Country Music*. He proceeds to quote Yoakam: "'If country music is going to gain the attention and respect of a young audience, they're going to have to address what I call the "emotional integrity" of the music,' he says. 'It's extremely important that honky-tonk music have youth involved in it . . . We have an opportunity to reclaim some ter-ritory and reintroduce it to those kids, that young audience.'"

Kingsbury asks: "Is middle America ready for Dwight Yoakam? The question is not as silly as it sounds, because by signing with a Nashville label, Yoakam is aiming himself squarely at working men and housewives, when his only proven audience has been young rock fans."

Dwight responds: "We are not cowpunk. We are a classic hillbilly act. That's what we do. We are a honky-tonk band. That being the case, this music has a natural and rightful kind of audience—in Sapulpa, Oklahoma; Louisville, Kentucky; Birmingham, Alabama; or Odessa, Texas. Those people understand it . . . We've achieved a certain teaching process with the young people we've been doing it for in L.A. And we had the opportunity to sign with a couple of West Coast labels. But country music is, was, and always will be the music of middle America."

If we leave a certain inscrutability of syntax aside ("achieved a certain teaching process"?), Dwight was ready to bring his music back home, to Ohio (and Kentucky), to the people he knew best. To confirm his convictions, country music would need to change. Significantly. Quickly. Like flooring a red-hot Corvette out of a deep rut. In the meantime, things were changing for Dwight in Los Angeles, where he'd long been ignored, had later been accepted, and was now starting to get a taste of what the life ahead might be like.

Remembers Dave Alvin, "Right before Dwight's Warner Bros. LP came out, he and I went to see George Strait at the Universal Amphitheatre. And suddenly this guy who had been playing to forty people at the Palomino has carte blanche backstage. And I realized that he is being groomed here. There's that grace period in the music industry, where three months before your album is released, and two weeks after it's released, everybody loves you. 'Cause they all know you may be the next big thing. 'Hey, man, can I get you a drink? My girlfriend? Fine, take her.' So we were totally 'in crowd' at this George Strait performance, and I felt totally out of place."

Dwight didn't, and this was a crucial difference between Yoakam and Dave Alvin, the Blasters, and pretty much anyone else who would attempt to find commercial stardom without sacrificing rootsy integrity. Dwight could straddle two worlds—be they hillbilly and Hollywood, punk rock and mainstream country, authenticity and flash—the way few others could. He blazed a trail that many others would try to follow, but they'd take a few steps and falter. He was somehow able to climb to the top.

"It's Jes' Ol' Hillbilly Stuff"

IN THE RECORDING STUDIO, Dwight Yoakam and the Babylonian Cowboys had become a finely tuned, well-oiled machine,
able to stop on a dime. Onstage, the band was a supercharged
muscle car with the potential to recklessly careen out of control (or at least create the illusion that they might). And they
drove the audience wild in the process.

If Dwight was sitting behind the steering wheel—de-
termining the course of his artistry through his songs, his
voice—Pete was riding shotgun. The latter's guitar plainly provided the pedal-to-the-metal acceleration, bringing a live-wire
charge to the performance that was only a hint in the recorded
arrangements. Impulse and adrenalin ignited his progressions,
as if the guitar were playing him, or playing *through* him.

But Dwight remained a master of reserve, in full command
of his craft, his vocal phrasings and shadings, the material he
wrote, even of the crowds that were growing larger and more

excited at the prospect of an emerging phenomenon. Though Pete's current could surge through Dwight as well, turning him into a whirling dervish during instrumental breaks, it was the tension between the two of them onstage—latent, laconic Dwight and kinetic, explosive Pete—that powered the pistons of this musical dynamic.

Where the first disc of the deluxe edition of *Guitars, Cadillacs, Etc., Etc.* documents the big leap that Dwight's music had made in the studio from the 1981 demos to the 1986 release of his major-label debut, the second disc provides even greater revelation. It's amazing in retrospect that it took two decades for this recording to see release, for if there is one document that could testify to the singularity of Dwight's significance, of his music's potential to merge the rawest rock with the most commercially successful country in a way no one had done before and hasn't since, this is it.

Recorded live at the Roxy on West Hollywood's Sunset Strip, a different world entirely from the Palomino in North Hollywood, it captures Yoakam and band as they prepare to widen their orbit, just weeks following the album's release. The launching pad wasn't a country club, and this wasn't a country crowd. The Roxy was the epicenter of neon hip in the capital of the entertainment industry, though to Nashville this scene meant little or nothing.

Thus, the performance found Dwight poised between two worlds—the roots-rock, cowpunk crowd of his recent past and the mainstream country audience of his immediate future. "Honky-Tonk Man" was already a debut hit single and power rotation video (featuring Dwight's own power rotation, charged by the twang), converting listeners who wouldn't have known the Blasters from the Beat Farmers into fans of the brash young artist whose old sound was the newest thing in country music.

It would soon be branded "neo-traditionalism" and turned into something of a movement, linking Yoakam with the likes of Steve Earle and Marty Stuart, who also brandished the "hillbilly" tag as a badge of honor. But Earle, despite his base in Nashville, was too ornery to find much favor with mainstream country after his *Guitar Town* album (released at the same time as Yoakam's debut), while Stuart never meant anything to rock fans. Only Yoakam made significant impact in both musical worlds.

After the Roxy show, recorded for broadcast on the *Live at Gilley's* program (an irony, for Gilley's was the Texas mega-tonk that had inspired the *Urban Cowboy* phenomenon to which Yoakam's music provided an antidote), Dwight Yoakam and the Babylonian Cowboys would hit the road for their debut headlining tour: crossing the country twice, then traversing the Atlantic to introduce themselves to Europe.

All but unknown on the Los Angeles club circuit just a few years earlier while juggling an assortment of odd jobs, Yoakam would be a conquering hero upon his return from this blitzkrieg ten-month tour, with a debut album that had topped the country charts and a live show that gave both country and rock fans something to rave about. He would be leaving clubs the size of the Roxy behind, playing for thousands rather than hundreds.

The Roxy set anticipated this phenomenon, combining the bravura of a band that knew it had captured lightning in a bottle with the excitement of a crowd that recognized it was on the ground floor of something big. Not to make too much of such comparisons, but think of the Beatles in Hamburg. The Ramones at CBGB. Elvis on *Louisiana Hayride*. Hank Williams . . . wherever Hank Williams flashed the raw intensity of the music that millions would soon come to know through more polished recordings.

In the words of Buck Owens, to whom Dwight would pay homage in his introduction to "Guitars, Cadillacs," Yoakam and his band had a tiger by the tail.

Almost twenty-five years later, his enthusiasm about that night remains undiminished, as we sit in his offices on Sunset Boulevard, just a short stretch down the hill from the club where he'd recorded his performance, the prime location of his business office and down-home opulence evidence of the success he'd enjoyed over the decades since. And this is when Dwight exclaimed, "When you listen to the Roxy Theatre, that bonus disc with the deluxe edition of *Guitars, Cadillacs*, that is the moment! We knew! We didn't know what we knew, but we knew. We knew we were headed somewhere."

The set starts with Pete's coiled riffing, generating tension through repetition, sustaining a dynamic that evokes rock's primal energy. Perhaps, in country ritual, Dwight isn't even onstage yet, letting the band warm the crowd's enthusiasm before the headliner's triumphant entrance. Or maybe he is, for there is no applause signifying an entrance. Instead, the fiddle of Brantley Kearns makes its presence known, marking a dramatic shift from rock club to hoedown, providing the frame for Dwight's high, lonesome vocals on "Can't You Hear Me Calling," the Bill Monroe classic that serves as his set opener.

The shift sets the parameters, establishing the common denominator for the music. For the band to be capable of rocking so hard, with the singer fronting it sounding so country, suggests a refusal to compromise in the manner of so much country rock, which had pulled its punches in a way that sounded hippie-dippy rather than authentically shit kicking or slam dancing. There was something dangerous in the music's synergy, as if its ability to inject punk-rock energy into honky-tonk tradition—to find common spirit in categories more often considered opposite polarities—was the aural equivalent of splitting the atom.

"We hadn't been concerned with contemporary country at all, because it was in a pretty ugly state," says Anderson. "Which seems funny to say now, because I'm not even sure that country exists any more. But we were just concerned with playing the way we played. We'd take off the radio what we liked, but there were enough honky-tonks out here to play what you wanted. And people dug it. So you could spend the whole night playing really good, hard-core stuff."

Though Pete had never considered himself a country player, Dwight was presenting himself as nothing but—an embodiment of country music returned to its pure, unvarnished state. With the contrast between the two powering the musical synergy, the Roxy set would underscore the crucial contradiction of Yoakam's career: the music could be so obviously real—undeniably so, in the power that surged back and forth between artist and audience, obliterating the wall between the two—while the performance was so obviously artifice.

Such an (obvious) observation isn't intended as criticism, though Yoakam's detractors would level it as such. For what is show business—if not all of popular culture—but artifice that is essential to the art? Some artists gleefully rub the consumer's nose in the contrivance—David Bowie, Madonna, Lady Gaga, even Bob Dylan—as if the manipulation of identity is the popular artist's real art.

Others invite the audience to engage in what noted rock critic Samuel Taylor Coleridge once termed "the willing suspension of disbelief." Whether it's Hank Williams donning the cowboy hat that was never in fashion in his native Alabama, or Bruce Springsteen celebrating his working-class authenticity long after he became a bicoastal millionaire, or the lionization of the Clash playing revolutionary guerrillas (backed by the promotional muscle of a mighty international media conglomerate), we believe what we want to believe, what the art convinces us to believe. And our beliefs are as fluid as the identities of the artists we come to embrace, for how else could an artist reviled as the ultimate sham (Johnny Cougar) reclaim himself as the embodiment of small-town, pink-houses authenticity (John Mellencamp)?

Whatever everyone involved believed on the night Yoakam gave his triumphant 1986 performance, it's hard to hear it now without recognizing that Dwight was putting on an act—that this intelligent, articulate man who had been raised in Columbus, Ohio, and attended his hometown Ohio State University was impersonating, a rube, a hayseed. And not just impersonating but exaggerating: "Wuhl, *thank* you. We're just *tickled* you came out tonight. Listen to yuhs carry on." And, later: "Now they're getting ugly, yelling stuff . . . acting like you're at a honky-tonk. On the *Sunset Strip*!"

So the audience was acting as well? Maybe they were all in on the act. Yoakam was acting as if he was a guy who had somehow fallen off the back of a turnip truck instead of an artist capable of conjuring a musical ethos that had been popular around the time he was born, a music that this audience had never experienced firsthand. And so the audience was acting as if Yoakam was a real honky-tonker—whatever that might mean amid the Hollywood glitz of the mid-1980s—and that the Roxy had transformed itself into a real honky-tonk. For one night at least.

Was there anything real in this? Of course, indisputably, as stated before, the galvanizing power of the music was real, particularly in comparison with the safe, sanitized version of contemporary country that had smothered that original hillbilly spirit. Or the rootless, multi-tracked arena rock that had no more spontaneity than the computers linking the keyboards to the lights. And the connection that Yoakam and band forged with the audience that night was as real as the musical muscle that had forged it. This was hardscrabble, angular artistry, music without fat or filler, music that felt like the real thing to an audience too late to have experienced the real thing. In an era of commercial calculation, there was nothing safe about it.

There's an apocryphal quote often (if ironically) attributed to Hank Williams: "The key to country music is sincerity. If you can fake that, you've got it made."

As Richard A. Peterson describes the phenomenon in his brilliant *Creating Country Music: Fabricating Authenticity* (University of Chicago Press, 1997), "Authenticity is not inherent in the object or event that is designated authentic but is a socially agreed-upon construct in which the past is to a degree misremembered." Which is exactly what Hank Williams would have meant, if he had ever said what he never said.

Within this "socially agreed-upon construct," we collectively ignore the obvious—that faking it, or putting on an act, is just another term for putting on a show. However authentic (or not) Dwight may have been, he was undeniably sincere. He sincerely wanted to be a star—a country rock star when that had seemed to be a possibility, a country star now that it wasn't, at least according to the formatted dictates of commercial radio. He sincerely refused to compromise his principles in order to achieve that goal of stardom. He sincerely fronted a smoking-hot band. And he sincerely thought that country music had strayed from its rightful path, that it had betrayed its better self politically, geographically, generationally, artistically.

And he sincerely believed, deep down in his bones, that his music represented a corrective—a power that could not be denied, a charisma that could not be ignored, a flash that obliterated any distinction between the real and the surreal. For what Dwight was conjuring was a parallel dimension, one where country music hadn't decamped to the suburbs, where rock and roll shared a common spirit with it, and where punk energy could be harnessed to restore something rather than destroy it. And where retro honky-tonk was the hippest new trend in Hollywood.

Throughout the performance, Dwight invoked the inspirations that his singular musical dynamic was channeling. There was Kentucky homeboy Bill Monroe, of course, who shared Dwight's audacity and had all but invented the music known as bluegrass, but whose stiff, autocratic demeanor was at odds with Yoakam's. There were Buck and Merle and the rest of the Bakersfield crowd, whose California legacy would come to provide such a strong imprint for Dwight's own, so much so that Buck would subsequently be perceived as Yoakam's main musical mentor, and Dwight would be known as the guy who had rescued Buck's reputation from *Hee Haw* corn.

And there were the two artists whom he'd acknowledged as the twin beacons of musical inspiration that had drawn him to California, both in attendance that night at the Roxy, as if passing the generational torch. Dwight toned down the hokum as he acknowledged their presence: "There's a couple of folks here tonight that were a big influence to me in the late '60s and early '70s . . . John Fogerty and Miss Emmylou Harris. I think you both gave a lot of people a lot of hope that there was still room for youth in country music."

There's revisionism in that tribute, because even Dwight acknowledges that when he first listened to Creedence, the hope the band's string of hits instilled was that there was room in *rock* for considerable country influence, that a young artist could synthesize the most powerful rock and the purest country into something other than the trifle that country rock had become. The initial goal had been mainstream rock success rather than anything to do with Nashville. And Emmylou's emergence with Gram Parsons initially made a much stronger imprint in rock circles than in country.

But even now that country stardom had become the quest, the frenzied response that Yoakam's music generated in live performance was like nothing Nashville had seen, nothing that Fogerty or Harris had experienced, nothing like what rock audiences too typically accepted. No, as the song that followed Yoakam's introduction underscored, this artist had bigger fish to fry. What's obvious in retrospect, even if it wasn't at the time, is that the main comparison to what Yoakam was doing was to Elvis Presley, circa '56, the year Dwight was born, the era when television so significantly extended the power of the music through its reach. The year of the swiveling hips.

Yoakam never mentioned Elvis Presley that night, but even before he and the band launched into "Mystery Train," following his nod to Fogerty and Harris, it was evident that the specter of Elvis hovered as powerfully over Dwight's music—and would through the years to come—as any of the rest of his more often acknowledged influences. From the time that Yoakam became a national breakthrough artist, early Elvis's essence and contradictions would most closely parallel his own: a Southern boy who had arrived out of nowhere to transform the musical landscape to his dictates, the one who combined rock's unbridled sexuality with courtly country manners—as if he were an animal in heat onstage and a gentleman in church off it. The artist who initially had no idea where his career trajectory would take him but who never lost touch with his mythical roots. The guy whose music combined rock and roll, rockabilly, country, blues (through Pete), aggressively sexual and transcendently religious elements into a seamless whole. The cultural rebel who conquered the mainstream. The guy whose hip shake drove the girls wild.

There are times—particularly in the breathy coda to his version of Hank Williams's "My Bucket's Got a Hole in It"— when Yoakam practically sounds like an Elvis impersonator.

Within this parallel dimension, Yoakam was Elvis in reverse. Where Elvis had been a rock and roll sensation belatedly embraced in his maturity by the Nashville country establishment, Yoakam was presenting himself from the outset as a country artist, albeit one with more rock and roll sizzle than most contemporary rock.

For those of us across the nation who knew Yoakam only from his recorded music—first the EP, then the LP—the tour following the Roxy date would not only confirm that he and the band could deliver the goods, but that the recordings barely provided a hint of the incendiary quality of Yoakam's music live. It's this spirit that burns through the Roxy recording, and which gave me my baptism by fire when Yoakam made his Chicago debut on that first tour.

It was a steamy June evening when Yoakam took the stage at the Vic, a restored theater that often brought cutting-edge rock acts to this hip neighborhood toward the south of Wrigleyville, but rarely country artists, particularly the type of artist likely to be played on country radio. (It would subsequently feature renegade Texans such as Joe Ely and Billy Joe Shaver as alternative country gained critical mass.)

Seeing Yoakam for the first time was like my first Clash concert. I was blindsided, because Yoakam's studio sessions gave little hint of the mayhem this music was capable of inspiring from the stage. Only in my imagination had I experienced one of those buckets-of-blood joints where the band played from behind chicken wire to protect the musicians in case the crowd got too boisterous and started tossing beer bottles.

The Vic was by no means that sort of club, and there was no danger of bottles being thrown. *But it felt like there was.* There was such wild, crazy energy to the music that it felt like anything could happen. And that Yoakam and his music were encouraging the crowd to let loose, egging them on.

In his 2011 memoir, *See a Little Light: The Trail of Rage and Melody*, renowned rocker Bob Mould remembers a similar dynamic when Yoakam opened for Hüsker Dü, Mould's stalwart Minneapolis band that drew a crowd that couldn't have contained a single mainstream country fan: "Our special support act . . . was Dwight Yoakam, who had just signed with Reprise Records, another Warner label. The punks down front were yelling at Dwight to play faster, and he handed the situation very well—by playing faster."

Well before conquering the country charts, Dwight had developed an unshakable confidence in the power of his music to turn skeptics into converts. I'd gone to the Vic show expecting to enjoy it—hell, I'd loved seeing Ernest Tubb and George Jones when they'd played more predictably suburban country venues before older, mind-your-manners crowds. But this was something entirely different, something unhinged. I left the show drained, spent, soaked with sweat. But cleansed in a way. Baptized, initiated. Knowing that I would never again hear traditional country music in quite the same way.

9

Hillbilly Deluxe

YOAKAM'S RECORD LABEL had been gun-shy about the "hillbilly" reference in what had belatedly become the title song of his debut album. But his instincts had paid such dividends that his sophomore album flaunted the term. Recorded just thirteen months after the debut's release, *Hillbilly Deluxe* represented the work of a successful, confident hitmaker with attitude to burn.

There's a cliché in the music industry that helps explain the dreaded "sophomore slump": you get your whole life to write your debut album, and then you get six months to scrape together material for your follow-up. Maybe you're rushed into the studio after writing feverishly from the road, trying to force yourself into creative mode for the second while you're still tirelessly hustling the first. Such a career pace can be a little like riding a rodeo bronco, and it's no wonder that so many get bucked off—if not for good, at least suffering some significant bumps and bruises in the process.

By contrast, Yoakam showed no sign of sophomore slump with the release of *Hillbilly Deluxe* in April 1987, following his first extended stint of hard touring as a headliner. Rather than succumbing to any pressure about following the chart-topping success of *Guitars, Cadillacs, Etc., Etc.*, he seemed even more cocksure.

"We were gold, going on platinum," remembers Pete of how much things had changed when it was time to record the follow-up. "When we started, Dwight had twenty-one songs that were really good, that we played on the bandstand. So I said to him, 'Let's do seven of your songs and three covers on every album. So right now you've got three albums' worth of material.' So he had 'South of Cincinnati,' 'I Sang Dixie,' and 'Johnson's Love' that were all slow tempo tunes. And it wasn't that any of them was basically better, but we couldn't put all three on the same record."

So *Hillbilly Deluxe* wasn't an album of leftovers, songs not considered quite as good as those on the debut. It was a triumph of selection and sequencing from an artist and producer who had already been thinking a couple moves ahead.

It shows an artist in full command of his music, his persona, his identity. Before he'd signed with Reprise, Yoakam had been a novelty, an anomaly, a cowboy hat on the Los Angeles punk circuit. Now he was quickly a mainstream country star, with an audience that had both changed dramatically and expanded exponentially through radio play, live performance, and video exposure. That last element would become as crucial in country music as it had already proven in pop rock, hastening the obsolescence of a wrinkled generation of performers (some of the same ones whose legacies Yoakam's music tapped into) for a younger, more videogenic stable of stars.

A child of television, Yoakam embraced the medium; he had been born to it. During the years before the advent of

Garth—whose country concerts would become as filled with special-effects spectacle as a Kiss extravaganza—there were already artists who could employ video as image enhancement and others who considered it a curiosity at best, a burden, a challenge, or even a corruption. On radio, some fans might have considered Dwight Yoakam and, say, Randy Travis, to be kindred, neo-traditionalist spirits. On video, they inhabited different planets.

As in rock, so many of those who emerged in video's wake had little to offer beyond looks. If they looked good, Nashville could make them sound good, at least by the commercial standards of country radio. Yoakam may have looked like a male model on the cover of his second album, head and hip cocked; jeans studded and fashionably torn; hat, coat, and bolo tie completing the requisite ensemble. The chip on his shoulder firmly in place, though invisible. But the music inside confirmed that he was the complete package. This was the work of an artist, producer, and band that knew exactly what they were doing.

There is more of a sense of direction here than on the debut, which had augmented his indie EP with four cuts subsidized by the label and subsequently recorded at Hollywood's Capitol Studios. Two of those four cuts, "Honky-Tonk Man" and "Guitars, Cadillacs" had given Yoakam his breakthrough hits. Those sessions had also marked the first time that Yoakam and Anderson would enlist the services in the studio of a third crucial collaborator, engineer Dusty Wakeman, whose role on subsequent releases would be elevated to associate producer.

Recalls Wakeman, "I met Pete and Dwight for the first time through the first *South of Bakersfield* record [an anthology of SoCal progressive country kindred spirits]. And they liked my work and wanted to record in L.A. with a rock engineer rather than going to Nashville, which was still in the very mellow

Urban Cowboy era. Now Nashville's a world-class recording center, but back then they kind of had one way of doing stuff, and that didn't include playing loud. And I was making punk records at the time, so I was used to that."

Not only did Yoakam and band have the confidence of an act that had achieved power rotation on the country airwaves and proven even more powerful on the concert stage, they still had a backlog of material. After all, their club residencies had required them to perform far more music than they could have ever squeezed onto the debut.

"This Drinkin' Will Kill Me," the kickoff track to the 1981 demos, became the album closer for *Hillbilly Deluxe*. It was as if the song had been held in reserve for the crucial second album that the success of the first would ensure. The smoking "Please, Please Baby" had long been a favorite with Yoakam's punk-rock fans. "Johnson's Love," which sounds like Yoakam's version of George Jones's classic "He Stopped Loving Her Today," is yet another song steeped in the Kentucky memories of his coal-mining grandfather, Luther Tibbs.

"'Johnson's Love' and 'South of Cincinnati' are both about my grandparents, but those songs have nothing to do with them, the facts of their lives," says Yoakam of these two songs about love's estrangement and endurance. "They were together forever, over fifty years. My grandfather is the central character in 'Johnson's Love,' but it's not him literally. It's just the tool that allows the writer to move beyond himself to something larger than himself. That's the task at hand. And that's what the best writing can be, using what you know to think beyond yourself."

As for the sense of direction that distinguishes album two from its predecessor, its signpost comes with its concluding acknowledgment on the liner credits: "VERY SPECIAL THANKS: to Buck Owens for all his records that still serve as an inspiration

for the California honky-tonk sound." Buck had been conspic-
uously absent from the list of country recordings that Yoakam
remembered hearing in his Ohio boyhood from his parents'
collection. (Like Merle Haggard, he was a Capitol recording
artist, so not as likely to be featured among the Columbia Record Club offerings as Johnny Horton, Stonewall Jackson, or
Marty Robbins.)

Neither the material nor the arrangements on Yoakam's
1981 demo betrayed much influence of Buck's Bakersfield
sound. Yet like all fans who came of musical age in the 1960s,
Dwight was familiar with Buck's music through the Top 40 success of "I've Got a Tiger by the Tail" and through the Beatles'
cover of his "Act Naturally." He had acknowledged Buck at the
Roxy performance as an influence among many. And, perhaps
most crucially, his teaming with Pete Anderson had found its
template in Owens's long-standing musical association with
guitarist Don Rich.

Just as Buck's diehard fans never spoke of his artistry without celebrating the crucial contributions of guitarist Rich, so
had Anderson established himself as Yoakam's essential foil,
with the assertive voice of his guitar in frequent call-and-
response duet with Dwight's lead vocal. Anderson was not
only the architect of Yoakam's arrangements, his guitar was
the lead element within them.

Whatever Owens's influence had been implicit in Yoakam's
music became explicit with the kickoff track to *Hillbilly Deluxe*.
"Little Ways," one of four of the ten tracks on the album that
would become a Top 10 country hit, is distinctly an homage
to Buck, a signature combination of the drawn-out phrasing
and hard-twanging guitar that had distinguished so many of
his hits. With the album's dedication and kickoff track, Yoakam seemed to be connecting himself to Owens as directly as
Asleep at the Wheel had to Bob Wills or early Aerosmith had

to the Rolling Stones. "Little Ways" was a new number written by Dwight, but it was unmistakably a Buck Owens song. After this, it would be harder to think of Yoakam as anything other than an Owens acolyte.

"Most of the album was what the band did live, but they were trying to capture a sound in the studio, that Bakersfield sound, an updated version," says Wakeman. "Because Buck and the Buckaroos had played the Fillmore and stuff like that. When they played live, they played hard and loud. They were rockin'."

For Dave Alvin, Yoakam's earliest influential fan, those two albums are the ones that fulfill the promise he had seen in Dwight the first time he heard him at the Palomino: "To me, those are the two impact albums. He walked up to the plate and hit a couple of home runs. And then he may have hit some triples and doubles, and a couple home runs after that, but those are the first two—the rookie goes up and bats it out of the ballpark. And part of the charm of Dwight in the early days was the band. Those two records sounded like a band playing band music. It was a motherfucker band. And that's hard to keep up over the course of a career."

Whatever calculation went into Yoakam's success distinguished him from Alvin's Blasters and most of their brethren on the roots-rock circuit that had given Dwight his first audience. It was a mark of integrity in that crowd not to care too much—about your presentation, about your commercial prospects, about anything more than the rush of the night's performance, getting yourself and your audience off. Dwight had his eyes on the bigger picture. He knew where he was going and how he was going to get there.

"Everything that I wasn't, he was," says Alvin. "He was a good-looking guy, he was smart about his career. I'm a meat-eating, cigarette-smoking drinker. And I don't plan things.

People I've known who become big stars tend to have five-year plans. Even before Dwight signed to Warner, when we'd be out drinking—I'd drink and Dwight would get drunk [on the intoxication of his own projected future, while leaving the alcohol to Alvin]—he would tell me what songs were gonna be on his second album. And he was pretty close to right. Where me, I don't even know what songs are gonna be on the album I'm in the middle of working on. So he was always driven like that, and people who are that driven either fail miserably or succeed very well."

Failing miserably was never an option for Yoakam. Now that he'd captured the attention of mainstream country without losing his foothold in the cutting-edge, roots-rocking camp, Yoakam delivered a follow-up that achieved a perfect balance—between traditional and original material, between pensive balladry and frenzied rockers, between the dynamism of the live performance and the subtleties that distinguished Yoakam as a vocalist (and continued to provide the essential tension between his laconic understatement and the live-wire charge of Anderson's guitar).

The first single provided a double-barreled jolt, with a cover of Elvis Presley's "Little Sister" backed with Yoakam's own "This Drinkin' Will Kill Me." For those who would peg Yoakam as a country traditionalist, a honky-tonk anachronism, the Elvis connection not only reinforced the smoldering sexuality Yoakam exuded on the cover of *Hillbilly Deluxe*, it reminded us that Elvis had come to fame as the original "hillbilly cat," well before he was crowned the King of Rock and Roll.

Presley would remain a reference point throughout Yoakam's career, but another cover proved every bit as prophetic, as Yoakam and Anderson revived Lefty Frizzell's "Always Late with Your Kisses," which found the arrangement pushing the countrypolitan envelope toward the extreme of classic kitsch.

The highlight of the arrangement has Yoakam, Anderson, and Wakeman crooning the "always late" background chorus like modern day Jordanaires. Whatever the punk crowd would have thought of it, these guys were obviously having some fun in the studio and refusing to take themselves too seriously. If hard-core honky-tonk was fastball music, high and hard, up and in, this arrangement threw the audience a roundhouse curve. It wouldn't be the last time.

For all of Yoakam's uncompromising instincts, he wasn't a purist, one of those self-righteous preservationists who embalm in the name of revival. If there be complexities and contradictions between the hardest of hard twang and corniest of kitsch corn, well, let them be. You couldn't come of age in the era of television and AM radio without being something of an eclectic, a magpie.

I met Yoakam for the first time in the wake of *Hillbilly Deluxe*, and the encounter left me surprised, delighted, and confounded. Offstage, he felt little need to play the part, look the part, act the part. When we convened for an interview in the lobby café of Chicago's very posh and un-honky-tonkish Ritz-Carlton Hotel, I had to look twice when he came down from his room to make sure I recognized him. Sure, the jeans were tight, but tight jeans were the fashion of a generation, not a stage costume.

It was the ball cap that threw me, emblazoned with the logo of the Houston Colt .45s, who had long since changed their name to the Astros. (Dwight later explained that he favored the cap not only because it was more Old West than New Frontier, but because 45 evoked r.p.m., those singles with the big holes.)

I'd never even seen a picture of Dwight without some sort of cowboy hat, which reinforced his image as the lean, laconic cowboy—the strong, silent type. So I was hardly prepared for this chatterbox who would bend my ear for more than two hours, until we had exhausted both the patience of our wait-ress and what I'd thought would be an oversupply of blank tape. He had a lot to say about honky-tonk and hillbilly music (which he loved with a passion) and about Nashville (which he treated with suspicion), but he also had plenty to say about popular culture and literature and baseball and everything else under the sun.

You'd ask him a question and then you'd listen to the mono-logue unfold, unwind, in thinking-out-loud fashion that was usually incisive, often intriguing, given to flights of creative fancy. Any interviewer knows to save the tough questions for last (because if the first question is too challenging, it may well be the last), so by the end of the interview we'd established such a rapport—him talking, me listening—that I hit him with it: would he take off his cap? Could I see what he was hid-ing under there?

Not that I really cared about the state of his locks (or lack thereof), but his response would be indicative of how closely he guarded his image. He smiled and tipped it without hesi-tation. Yes, Dwight Yoakam had a thinning, receding hairline that might have undermined his image as a sex symbol, though he was far from going bald. But the real revelation was that he had no problem showing a reporter who'd been a stranger just a couple hours earlier that there was a distinct difference be-tween onstage Dwight and offstage Dwight, and that the latter had no confusion about which was which.

In subsequent years, Dwight was inevitably linked in the press with a number of high-profile romantic partners, some of whom may have simply wanted the publicity (and maybe he did as well). One of them later complained about Dwight's van-ity, that it took him so long to get ready to go anywhere, that he spent far more time in front of the mirror than she did.

The guy on the cover of *Hillbilly Deluxe* looks like the sort of pretty boy who would spend a lot of time in front of the mirror. The artist I interviewed at the Ritz was a regular guy who was talking too much and too fast to calculate how he was coming across or to care much. And like any journalist blessed with such a surfeit of material, I appreciated him all the more for it. As for vanity, he was willing to reveal what was underneath the baseball cap. Cheap Trick's Rick Nielsen, nobody's idea of a sex symbol (and a songwriter whose "I Want You to Want Me" subsequently provided a left-field hit for Yoakam), never would.

Streets of Bakersfield

NOW THAT YOAKAM had transcended the dreaded sophomore slump, as if the possibility of such a setback could have ever occurred to him, his third album found him at a pivotal juncture. Almost a quarter century later, the question remains whether 1988's *Buenas Noches from a Lonely Room* represents the culmination of something, the final ascent to the top of this particular peak, or the beginning of a new musical adventure.

Yoakam leans toward the former. "I look at it this way— those albums are trilogies, in a sense, in retrospect," he says of his musical progression. "It's like, I told 'em what I was gonna tell 'em [on *Guitars, Cadillacs, Etc., Etc.*]. I told 'em [on *Hillbilly Deluxe*]. And then I told 'em what I'd just told 'em [on *Buenas Noches from a Lonely Room*]. And so in the first trilogy, I was telling 'em where I'd come from, the legacy and culture that shaped my music."

Dusty Wakeman agrees, "The first three albums through *Buenas Noches*, that was a band playing their set, basically."

If that was how it looked from the inside, an outside perspective is that Yoakam's third release has some radical differences from the first two. It's the first to feature a personnel shift in the Babylonian Cowboys, with the departures of bassist J.D. Foster and fiddler Brantley Kearns. After two albums with a stable lineup, half the band from the clubs was gone, leaving only producer-guitarist Anderson and drummer Jeff Donavan, with new bassist Taras Prodaniuk, mandolinist Scott Joss, and keyboardist Skip Edwards (previously credited as an "honorary" Babylonian Cowboy) now listed as members of the expanded band.

Though such changes might only be noticeable to close readers of liner notes, the sessions also featured a couple of ringers whose key contributions would give Dwight the first chart-topping single of his career. The song was "Streets of Bakersfield," and the guests were Buck Owens and Tex-Mex accordion kingpin Flaco Jiménez. The latter's virtuosic progressions added an element never previously heard on Yoakam's records, though Jiménez was already well known among roots-music aficionados for his work with Doug Sahm and Ry Cooder. He would subsequently reunite with Sahm in the Grammy-winning Texas Tornados, and he was as synonymous with Tex-Mex conjunto music as Clifton Chenier was with Louisiana zydeco. In other words, he was musical royalty, but a stranger to mainstream country.

Most significantly for country music, this was the album that brought Buck Owens out of musical semi-retirement and back to the top of the charts for the first time in sixteen years, reinforcing a relationship between artists of different generations that seemed less like mentor and acolyte than father and son. Even their names had a soundalike quality to them (DWIGHT YOAK-am, BUCK OW-ens). The pairing proved so successful that Owens went on tour as Yoakam's special guest, where he received a regal welcome from a generation of fans who knew him only as legend (or from *Hee Haw*), while reinforcing a passing-the-torch claim to Yoakam's honky-tonk ascendance.

Underscoring the music's lineage and the album's rite-of-passage significance, studio musicians additionally included steel guitarist Tom Brumley, an alumnus of Buck Owens's Buckaroos, and Dobroist Al Perkins, a former member of the Flying Burrito Brothers. Among the emerging generation were harmony vocalists Jim Lauderdale and Randy Weeks of the Lonesome Strangers. It was as if a like-minded musical community had coalesced around Dwight Yoakam, and his artistry now stood for something bigger than itself.

Yet Yoakam's higher profile and legitimization by the blessing of Buck Owens sparked a backlash in some critical quarters. Writing in the *Village Voice*, rock critic (and Bruce Springsteen biographer) Dave Marsh said that sharing the stage with Owens "exposed Yoakam's hokum. Dwight's voice is richer and stronger than Buck's, and he has considerable obnoxious, ass-twitching stage presence. Yet everything he does is hyper-calculated . . . all part of the pose."

Such is the age-old authenticity argument, as if there's a dichotomy between a calculated and "natural" performance, as if Bruce Springsteen hadn't also showcased his butt (on album covers and video) in some pretty tight and expensive jeans. As if these charges weren't the same ones Elvis Presley had stared down. Perhaps a crucial difference was that Yoakam, like Elvis, was perceived as pandering to a female audience (and everyone knew that anything that made girls squeal couldn't be taken too seriously), while Springsteen retained his reputation as a man's man.

Marsh, again: "Yoakam, who pranced on at nine, wearing butt-hugging jeans and a Stetson pulled over his eyes . . ." Stetson be damned, real men don't prance. Or pose.

Producer Pete Anderson put a different spin on Yoakam's increasingly common practice of turning his butt to the audience. "Back when I was growing up in Detroit, the hottest act around was Billy Lee and the Rivieras, who later became Mitch Ryder and the Detroit Wheels," he told journalist Todd Everett ("Dwight Yoakam: Not Just Another Hat Act," *Journal of Country Music*, Vol. 15, No. 3). "As each show began, they'd come out onstage and perform the entire first number with their back to the audience. I never forgot that image, of the defiant attitude it conveyed."

Whatever Yoakam's sins of authenticity, they didn't seem to bother the venerable Alvis Edgar Owens Jr., himself a reinvented transplant to California (from Sherman, Texas). Nobody knew better how contrived this business could be than the *Hee Haw* host who had built a multi-million-dollar, multimedia empire (publishing, radio, TV, et al.) by putting a rube's mask over the mind of a canny businessman.

Not only had Buck's work with Don Rich provided inspiration for the musical dynamic between Dwight Yoakam and Pete Anderson, but he had provided a road map for how a renegade artist could conquer country music from a California outpost far removed from Nashville, and how a guy who presented himself as unsophisticated could prove time and again that he was the smartest man in the room.

Buck was nobody's fool, and neither was Dwight. That some critic (or many critics, almost all of them middle-aged males) might criticize a showman for putting on a show suggested just how out of touch such scribes were with the nature of show business. Born in the year of the Elvis scare, Dwight had come of age with televised guitar slingers, and he made no apology for trying to excite others in the way that such performers had excited him.

"Every performer has a public presentation," he insists. "It's *performance* of the material. It's like saying J.J. Cale [the laid-back Oklahoma artist whose songs are better known in renditions by Eric Clapton] might have had a better career as a recording artist if he'd had a better way to publicly perform other than sitting around an amp, hidden. That's not going to do much for your career as a public performer. They are distinct environments, and they require distinct abilities. Hopefully you have the talent to present your music. Think of Elvis or the Beatles without their ability to present themselves. There were arguably equally great writers at the time the Beatles hit, but they didn't present themselves like the Beatles did, those four guys at that moment . . .

"Attitude is what everything from Elvis Presley forward was. Delivery was an integral part of the validity of musical performance," Yoakam continues. "And when color exploded on television, it sure was exciting. It's like saying, 'Do you really need color?' Well, I guess you don't [he laughs]. You could just use that graphite stick. But Kandinsky over there has got some crazy stuff going on. Don't know whether you want to compete with that. It was a jet-age world. It's really that moment that shifts postwar America into supersonic gear."

With Yoakam himself shifting into supersonic gear, his teaming with Buck, the chart-topping single and album, the triumphant tour all seemed to elevate Dwight's stature—as if he was no longer emulating his heroes but had joined their ranks. To many listeners, "Streets of Bakersfield" might have seemed like a new song, maybe even a Yoakam original. It had in fact been recorded by Owens in the early '70s but never released as a single, buried instead as a track on his 1973 album, *Ain't It Amazing, Gracie*.

Yoakam had previously solicited Buck's seal of approval by arranging a meeting with him a year earlier and inviting him to guest with Dwight at a local fair performance, an invitation that Owens had surprisingly accepted. The bond led to their teaming in the recording studio, and the subsequent hit reinforced the blood ties of their artistry.

"Not since Don Rich had Buck felt such a kinship with a young musician, and he and Dwight became fast friends," writes Eileen Sisk in *Buck Owens: The Biography*. "Buck told A&E *Biography*, 'Dwight should have been one of my sons.'"

My *No Depression* colleagues David Cantwell and Bill Friskics-Warren included the hit in their *Heartaches by the Number: Country Music's 500 Great Singles* (at #361). Writes Friskics-Warren, "Nothing Dwight Yoakam has recorded better captures his outsider ethos than his 1988 duet with Buck Owens. 'I came here looking for something I couldn't find anywhere else,' Dwight declares to open the record, and despite the fact that Buck first sang the line sixteen years earlier, it's plain that Yoakam identifies with it as if it were telling his own story. Which, of course, it was."

He subsequently writes of Yoakam's early rejection in Nashville and pilgrimage to the West Coast, "He found north Hollywood's cowpunk scene much more receptive to his expansive artistic vision, which wed country and rock, hungering to see how far each could bend without breaking. It's an approach certainly evident here, as Yoakam and producer Pete Anderson reinvent Owens's sprightly original as a slashing, accordion-driven polka worthy of L.A.'s post-punks Los Lobos."

While the album remains best remembered for the hit with Owens and Jiménez, it also represents a distinct departure from Yoakam's previous work, away from the *audio verité* of the bandstand (despite Wakeman's assertion) for a more cinematic expanse that would mark his subsequent artistic progression.

You might not know it from Flaco's uptempo accordion, but the material is almost relentlessly bleak, occasionally lethal, a descent into the depths of honky-tonk hell.

It's a mark of the contradiction and complexity that contributed to Yoakam's mystique that the album escalating his commercial triumph was also the darkest of his career, pushing past the heartbreak that had always been a cry-in-your-beer honky-tonk tradition into more dangerous, edgier territory. He marks that emotional terrain with the opening "I Got You," which passes as a love song only in the "thank heaven for small favors" sense, with the singer mainly recounting what he hasn't got, in terms of financial security.

"Hey, I know my life seems a mess," he sings over the hard twang of Anderson's guitar and the bare bones of the production. "But, honey, things to me still look real swell. 'Cause I've got you to see me through. Yeah, I've got you to chase my blues. I've got you to ease my pain. Yeah, I've got you, girl, to keep me sane."

Such meager consolation is conspicuous by its absence through the rest of the album, with was plainly envisioned as a cohesive song cycle (like the releases of the most ambitious rock artists) rather than a collection of hits and filler (which was more the country norm). The title aside, this is no *buenas noches*, but a dark night of the musical soul. The brooding title ballad, perversely released as a single, ends on this cheery note: "In the cold morning silence I placed the gun to her head. She wore red dresses, but now she lay dead."

A lyric worthy of Raymond Chandler, it comes after a pair of cheating songs, "One More Name" and "What I Don't Know" ("might get you killed"). Within such a context, the covers of Johnny Cash's "Home of the Blues" and Lazy Lester's "I Hear You Knockin'" might sound comparatively cheery, though the lyrics of both reinforce the emotional bleakness. "It's too late, baby," he sings in the latter, an inspired choice for an artist pigeonholed as a country purist. "Your calling is all in vain."

The album also makes the final dips into the 1981 demo, for the skid-row lament of "I Sang Dixie" and the equally funereal "Floyd County." The former had been the only song to spark a smattering of interest in Nashville, in Yoakam as a songwriter but not as singer. After it never ended up on that Hank Williams Jr. album, it provided Dwight with a follow-up chart topper to "Streets of Bakersfield" (which, if you listen to the lyrics, is equally down in the mouth).

Says Pete Anderson, "'I Sang Dixie' I'd always set a little bit aside, because I thought it was his best song. And I didn't want to put it on the first or even the second album, because I thought this is a number one record. And you've got to beat the doors down with the other material so that they're ready to listen to you."

As for the album's thematic cohesiveness, Anderson didn't necessarily hear it the way that Dwight did (or I do): "Dwight went into the third record and, in his mind, he made it a theme record. I don't know if some of it's thematic, but you don't really care what someone's motivation is. Five or six of those songs had been written for quite awhile. And he slid in 'She Wore Red Dresses' and a couple of other things that made it a thematic record—in his mind. I just looked at it as a collection of really good songs that worked together."

After all of the album's scuffling, woe, heartbreak, and lethal revenge, it concludes with a two-song coda of sorts, in tribute to the homefolks. Reunited with Maria McKee (now that Dwight was the star and Lone Justice had gone nowhere), they revive Hank Locklin's "Send Me the Pillow," the song he remembers his mother and aunt "bellerin'" at the record player. He follows that with "Hold on to God," a rare reflection in his recording career of his formative days in church, "written and performed for my mother, Ruth Ann."

Dwight summarized the album's narrative progression to *Billboard* (October 15, 1988): "I get moody. I kill someone. Then I get religion in the end. This record's more me—there are expressions of me that people have never heard before."

They'd soon learn just how much more there was to Dwight than the honky-tonk traditionalism that had been his calling card. This was his third straight album to top the country charts. It would also be his last. Yet Yoakam's artistic vistas would continue to expand as his popular profile rose. There was a whole wide world to conquer beyond the conventional strictures of country music.

Bonus Cut

NOTHING DISTINGUISHED the difference between rock and country recording artists more than the greatest hits album. Since the late 1960s and early '70s, rock had primarily been an album-driven music, while hit singles remained the currency of country. Since other tracks that hadn't been designed for single release were plainly filler, country fans who wanted the most for their dollar often waited until the artist had enough hits to warrant a compilation of those singles.

Such collections in rock circles were (like live albums) seen as signs that the artist needed a creative breather, was switching labels, or was nearing the end of a commercially successful string. Thus, they typically came later in a rock artist's career, though, even in country, it was uncommonly early for an artist to package his greatest hits after only three releases.

Then again, Dwight had already had a lot of chart success, enough to warrant the release of *Just Lookin' for a Hit* in

September 1989. And perhaps he needed a creative breather as well, a chance to replenish the stockpile of original material now that the 1981 demo had finally been exhausted (except for "Please Daddy").

For all of his radio success, Dwight was among a "raised on rock" generation of emerging country artists, ones who paid attention to albums as coherent wholes rather than hit-and-miss selections of singles and filler. Steve Earle, Rosanne Cash, (her then husband/producer) Rodney Crowell, Lyle Lovett, Nanci Griffith, and others who were enjoying success or were attempting to establish themselves as country artists in the pre-Garth period all carefully conceived of albums as albums. Not necessarily concept albums, with which Johnny Cash, Merle Haggard, and Willie Nelson had previously built artistic parameters beyond country convention, but albums that held together as albums.

To trace the careers of such artists through a succession of singles would be sketchy, incomplete. And so it was with Yoakam, who had been conceiving of each album as an album, paying particular attention to the sequencing of material as well as the selection of it. But the market must be served, and the country market dictated that an artist with enough hits must package them into a greatest-hits compilation, bringing potential fans to the cash register that had previously restricted their consumption of the artist's music to the radio.

Another convention of the greatest-hits album is that it should have at least one track available for the first time—a hoped-for hit-to-be, or something to make the diehard who already had all of this music on album buy the hits package as well. And here's where Yoakam threw his fans and the Nashville music establishment another curve ball, kicking off the collection of otherwise familiar material with "Long White Cadillac."

It was an inspired choice on multiple levels. As an account of the last night in the life of Hank Williams, it reinforced Dwight's connection to another outsider Nashville had never embraced and to musical values to which contemporary country barely paid lip service. As a number well known to fans of the Blasters, it showed that Yoakam hadn't forgotten that formative stage of his career and the L.A. roots-punk crowd that had embraced him when Nashville wanted nothing to do with him. And as one of the many great songs written by Dave Alvin, it would put some cash into the pocket of a benefactor who had recognized Yoakam's potential when few others did and who had given his career a crucial boost.

The years since had seen the former running buddies follow divergent career trajectories and pretty much lose touch with each other. After Dwight, Warner Bros./Reprise would also sign the Blasters and Los Lobos. And though the Blasters had been club kingpins in Los Angeles, both Yoakam and Los Lobos would reap far more national success than the Blasters ever did. Critics had long hailed Alvin as one of America's greatest roots-oriented songwriters since Creedence's John Fogerty (reinforcing the Yoakam-Alvin connection), but critics got their records for free.

A contentious relationship with his older brother Phil—who fronted the band and gave voice to Dave's songs—a desire to explore different musical avenues, and perhaps some commercial frustration would push Dave to split from the band. Though it seemed like the Blasters were going nowhere, commercially at least, Dave's solo career (after a brief stint in X) had difficulty gaining traction as well.

"So, I'd quit the band, I'd done a record on Epic, and to make a long story short, I was about forty grand in debt, living hand to mouth," remembers Alvin. "And I get a phone call from Dwight saying, 'I'm cutting "Long White Cadillac."' And

I saw a yacht in my future! And whatever anger I'd had at the record industry dissipated. It was a lifesaver. I'd sold almost all my guitars at that point.

"And he said, 'We're cutting it down at Capitol, you want to come down to the session?' And I went, 'Fuck yes!' So I went on down there, and they'd already cut the track and Dwight was putting on harmony vocals. As I'm driving over, I'm kind of imagining how it's gonna work as a country shuffle. And then I get there and hear this six-minute long psychedelic thing! And all I could do was think like a radio programmer—can we add more fiddle? [He laughs heartily.] Maybe shorten it a little? I'm trying to get a yacht here. Maybe just a rowboat.

"And Dwight said to me, 'This is my *fuck you* to country radio.' And my innermost thought was, 'Could you pick someone else's song to do that with?' [Alvin laughs again.] I could really use the money! But in hindsight, it was a great thing. It's probably his rockingest track, and I'm very proud of it. He was very sweet. The return favor was extremely appreciated."

At five and a half minutes long and with a harder-rocking arrangement than country radio could tolerate, Dwight's version of "Long White Cadillac" would never be a hit. But the album was, charting top three, and each one of those album sales put some royalty money in Alvin's pocket. Dwight insists that he never thought that cutting the track was repaying a favor.

"I did it because I loved that song," he says with a smile. "I thought it was one of the greatest songs ever written. A rock and roll homage to Hank Williams, who was essentially the first rock star. He was a hillbilly singer, but he was a rock star. As Chet Atkins said, the year that Elvis hit, it ruined country music. Because they had rural America and southern America's teenage audience. And then they couldn't keep them. Elvis had changed everything."

12

"Well, I'm Back Again . . ."

ONE OF THE REWARDS of immersing yourself in a project like this is the revelation of retrospect. I would have initially been tempted to give *If There Was a Way* short shrift, in comparison with the albums that frame it, because it hadn't left an indelible impression like *Buenas Noches* had nor had it issued an artistic proclamation the way *This Time* would. And its packaging had Dwight looking even more like a male model, striking poses that would make Madonna envious (from "come hither" on the back to the chain-link crucifixion in the booklet).

But when I listened to it with fresh ears after a couple decades of neglect, I was impressed by its durability, its depth, its quality. It features some of Yoakam's strongest writing and most subtly soulful singing, and it finds Anderson and the band bringing a creative renewal to the arrangements. At various stages of this writing, I'd find recurrent tunes running through my brain, then I'd hear the hooks of "The Distance

Between You and Me" or "Turn It On, Turn It Up, Turn It Loose" or "It Only Hurts When I Cry" or the title track, and I'd remember that they all came from this one album that I'd previously dismissed.

It was released in October 1990, more than two years after *Buenas Noches*, almost twice as long as Yoakam had previously gone without issuing an album of new, original material. And with the hits package as a stopgap that marked the end of something (an era, a chapter, a decade) for Yoakam, *If There Was a Way* almost demanded to be perceived as the start of something new.

But what? Instead of focusing, like its cohesive and cinematic predecessor had, it offered a little something for everyone, or at least for every faction of Dwight fandom. It was less a road map toward a musical destination than a Rorschach test where you could hear what you wanted. And if you thought of yourself as more of a country purist who preferred Dwight the traditionalist, Yoakam had never sounded more like classic country than he did on about half the album, while on the other half he offered a rapprochement of sorts with musical Nashville by co-writing for the first time on record (standard practice in Music City) and recording outside material by contemporary writers rather than reviving country chestnuts.

So you might say that this album found Dwight behaving and sounding more like a conventional country artist than he had in the past. Yet the album also showed him expanding his aural vistas, with the Hammond B-3 organ on the title track sounding a whole lot more like Muscle Shoals or Memphis than Nashville.

"That title track is Percy Sledge!" agrees Yoakam. "It's really an R&B groove, where we introduced the Hammond B-3 for the first time. That's soul, that's Stax. And I that's where I said, 'Here we go . . .'"

Prominently featured on background vocals throughout were Emily Saliers and Amy Ray, better known as the Indigo Girls, alt-folk lesbians whose status as Lilith Fair darlings made for an unlikely but inspired match with Dwight's brand of honky-tonk. David Leonard, who mixed the album (and would often work on subsequent Yoakam albums), had previously been celebrated for his credits with Prince.

As for the closing, workmanlike cover of "Let's Work Together," written by Wilbert ("Kansas City") Harrison—a 1970 hit for Canned Heat, subsequently reworked by Roxy Music's Bryan Ferry—it mainly served to show that there were interpretive limits to what Dwight could do. He was far more convincing when brooding about dark nights of the soul than celebrating the brotherhood of man.

Whatever the musical direction, Dwight's material rarely veered from the thematic road on which true love never runs smooth. His hit co-write of "It Only Hurts When I Cry" with the legendary Roger Miller holds its own with the best songs of either, and in it Dwight adapts the phrasing of an Elvis impersonator to a lyric steeped in reversal and denial: "The only time I feel the pain is in the sunshine or the rain. And I don't feel no hurt at all, unless you count when teardrops fall."

He tries a similar strategy with a more contemporary co-writer, the Nashville hitmaker Kostas, with "Nothing's Changed Here," which mainly details how everything changes after a lover's departure. Kostas also contributes the signature "Well, I'm back again . . ." on "Turn It On, Turn It Up, Turn Me Loose," making this the first album in which Dwight sang new songs that he didn't write, but sound like he could or should have.

Yoakam recalls that producer Pete Anderson brought the tune to him, saying, "People don't realize that your writing is your strength, and so they throw covers for you to do. But this is one song I've come across that sounds like something you would have written for yourself."

And then Dwight starts strumming and singing a snippet: "'Well I'm back again . . .'—with that Johnny Cash melodic moment, but then it gets a little more lilting. Like me."

Beyond collaborating with and covering songwriters from Nashville, Dwight seemed to make another concession to commercial country convention with his duet with country songstress Patty Loveless on "Send a Message to My Heart," the third song on the album that bore the Kostas imprint. Though released as a single, it barely cracked the Top 40, and in retrospect seems more like a move by Loveless toward Yoakam's brand of creative independence rather than a commercial ploy by Dwight.

Throughout the rest, Yoakam showed he could make the heartbreak of love lost sound existential (the album-opening "The Distance Between You and Me"), metaphoric ("The Heart That You Own"), drunk and defiant ("Since I Started Drinking Again"), haunted (the soulful title track), and absolutely gorgeous, with the string-laden balladry of "You're the One." That song demonstrated that Yoakam hadn't exhausted his storehouse of early material, since it predates the 1981 demo (with an inspiration that reaches back to high school) but was inexplicably not recorded during those sessions.

It proved to be the album's highest charting country hit, though "Turn It On, Turn It Up, Turn Me Loose," "It Only Hurts When I Cry," and "The Heart That You Own" all joined it in the top ten (the last just barely and briefly). For all its variety, the album ranks with Yoakam's most consistent in terms of the inspired quality of his material.

In a cover story for *Country Music* (July–August 1991), Patrick Carr praises the album thusly: "as wonderfully non-countrypolitan, kick-ass classic as ever, and even more intelligent, vivid, and precise than his previous work. It sounds as if he's really powering up, really finding his groove and focusing his vision."

Says Pete Anderson, "Dwight wrote a plethora of new songs, mining new ground with all the things he had learned. Because up through *Buenas Noches*, like I've said, we'd had twenty-one of his songs to record, and he wrote some new songs along the way. But not a whole album of new songs. And Kostas had come into the picture. We were painting with a broader brush and more colors on our palette. We could be a little bolder in what we did and how we did it. We had the Hammond organ, and it was like, *Whaaat*?"

Yoakam had now released four albums (not including the hits compilation), each sharing a common ethos but all distinctly different. And none offered more than a taste of what would come next, when Yoakam would release the biggest and arguably the most ambitious album of his career two and a half years later.

THOUGH *IF THERE WAS A WAY* wasn't a game-changer in the way that 1993's *This Time* would prove to be, it did arrive during the year that would transform the world of country music. For 1990 was the Year of Garth, in what would prove to be the Decade of Garth. While Garth Brooks had emerged the previous year with his self-titled debut, which included four hits, including two chart toppers, that album gave little hint of what a behemoth he was destined to become.

With the one-two punch of 1990's *No Fences* and 1991's *Ropin' the Wind*, Brooks recast country music in his image with the same sort of impact that the Beatles had on rock and roll in 1964. In both cases, the popular triumph of such dominating artistry (and/or marketing) provided a line of demarcation between before and after.

Before Garth (and after *Urban Cowboy*), country music had experienced a creative renaissance, as progressive acts with some appeal to rock fans enjoyed considerable success in Nashville. The king and queen of that brief era were Rodney Crowell (whose 1988 *Diamonds and Dust* contained an unprecedented *five* number-one country hits) and Rosanne Cash (Johnny's daughter and Rodney's wife at the time), with Steve Earle, Lyle Lovett, Foster and Lloyd, the O'Kanes, Nanci Griffith, and others combining country airplay with a popular base that included fans of folk and rock and music that transcended category.

Thus, Before Garth (or B.G.), many artists found the door open, at least a sliver, between the smaller country community and the larger world of rock. After Garth (or A.G.) that door slammed shut again, while the comparative sizes of the musical communities shifted significantly. It no longer seemed to make much sense for Nashville to aspire for crossover success, as country itself became the most popular music on the airwaves and at the cash register. It attracted converts with the popular craze of line dancing (suburban disco with a twang) and the "Achy Breaky Heart" of Billy Ray Cyrus and the new generation of country hunks.

Credit changing demographics, credit changing musical trends (as pop stations began to feature more hip-hop, much to the disdain of listeners raised on classic rock), or credit Garth alone. Whatever the cause, the sales figures that were considered a success in '80s Nashville were dismissed as pocket change in the 1990s. According to the bible of country music history, *Country Music, U.S.A.* (third revised edition, by Jocelyn R. Neal and original author Bill C. Malone), "By 1996, Brooks's accomplishment of over sixty million album sales had been surpassed only by the Beatles and Billy Joel, but he had achieved this spectacular figure more rapidly than any other artist in any field of music."

After Garth, Nashville had little interest in trying to sell a few hundred thousand albums by Steve Earle or Lyle Lovett, both of whom were subsequently shifted from their label's Nashville base to its Los Angeles pop/rock division. Country radio was far more receptive to a new generation of artists who would dominate the charts A.G.—Tim McGraw, Alan Jackson, Brooks & Dunn (assembled with as much calculation as Dwight's beloved Monkees), Faith Hill (who later married McGraw), Shania Twain—than to the more independent, creative types who had somehow found country favor during those days when there didn't seem to be as much at stake.

Perhaps the only act that enjoyed commercial country favor A.G. with a rebellious attitude comparable to Dwight's was the Dixie Chicks. And we all know what happened to them, and how quickly country music would turn on them. With the exception of Toby Keith (who didn't exactly share Yoakam's demographic), the prototype for the emerging generation of country artists who appealed to the growing legions of self-styled suburban cowboys was the nice guy, the next-door neighbor, the type you'd invite over for beer and a backyard barbecue.

A comparative punk like Dwight had no interest in coming to your barbecue. And he wouldn't drink your beer. He would never be one of the guys, in the way that Garth or Tim would, and not just because he was a teetotaling vegetarian. Garth was a marketing revolutionary who worked within the system as a recording artist, releasing the requisite album a year, glad-handing radio, press, and fans alike, while bringing a level of spectacle to the performing stage that had long been common in rock but provided a jolt to the country circuit. Dwight was one of the few holdover artists whose live performance was already electrifying enough to hold its own in the new era.

Another distinguishing difference between the rock and country worlds, where Dwight was the rare artist who sustained commercial and critical impact in each, is that rock had long ago splintered into a variety of different formats, from alt to classic and a number of niches in between, where country remained in the stranglehold of its equivalent of Top 40.

Both Before and After Garth, if you were on country radio, you were country. If you weren't, you weren't. Despite attempts to develop more progressive formats—with "adult alternative" and "Americana" initially sharing some of the same artists—the results were commercially marginal, even negligible. Former country hitmakers of the '80s and emerging artists classified as "alt-country" (which was really more of a rock category than one that the country industry acknowledged) often found their most influential airplay support from NPR stations, where listeners who might never have listened to country radio responded to the literacy of the songwriting and the "authenticity" of the musical roots.

Many of the artists cast adrift by country radio found creative emancipation and new audiences, even new artistic identities, now that they no longer had to feed the Nashville radio beast with singles that weren't likely to get played anyway. Johnny Cash, Emmylou Harris, and Rodney Crowell were among those who responded with their most inspired work in years. If they'd still been aiming for country radio, Cash wouldn't have covered Nine Inch Nails, nor would Harris have worked with alchemist producer Daniel Lanois (U2, Peter Gabriel), nor would Crowell have developed such a devastatingly confessional voice.

Yet Yoakam wasn't about to give up on country radio, nor was country radio going to give up on him. His ambitions, both creative and commercial, were too big for Americana or NPR. Since the era when he might have been a country-rock artist was ancient history, he would need to be a country star. Or a rock star. Or both.

"The Americana world is great, but you're not gonna put your kids through college and retire by selling Americana records," says Dusty Wakeman. "Our joke was that in Americana, five thousand is gold and ten thousand is platinum." (Within the commercial music industry, a sale of half a million units is gold, and a million is platinum.)

With *If There Was a Way*, Yoakam had planned to sustain his mainstream country success and he had succeeded. But he had also provided hints of plenty of possibilities beyond commercial country. And he subsequently positioned himself for a very different market with the 1992, Europe-only release of *La Croix D'Amour*.

"The Cross of Love" (a thematically appropriate evocation of Yoakam's music to date) is one of the more curious albums of Yoakam's career, though it doesn't even exist as far as his American recording career is concerned. Mainstream country success meant little in Europe, which responded to roots-oriented, rough-hewn, anti-hero American mavericks and considered Nashville polish a mark of artistic corruption.

According to Pete Anderson, the album was a result of the success Warner Bros. UK had enjoyed with time-warped rocker Chris Isaak, who had previously attracted only a cult following in the States. Yoakam and Isaak recognized each other as kindred spirits, though the former was categorized as country and the latter as rock. They were two California-based artists with a flair for retro (fashion, music, and otherwise), an affinity for twang, and a vision for an artistry that sounded timeless rather than anachronistic.

"This was the only time we ever took a curve ball from the record industry," says Anderson. "Chris Isaak had been having trouble breaking through in the States, but somebody at Warner Bros. in England had done something that really lit a fire for him over there. So then the suits in power thought, 'Wow, maybe we can do this with Dwight.' So we said, 'Okay, we'll play along, we'll be knuckleheads with you.' And that's what we did. It became knucklehead time.

"They asked everybody in the office to come up with a list of songs that they thought Dwight Yoakam should sing," he continued. "And they're in England, for Christ's sake. Some nineteen-year-old secretary is picking songs for the next album. And Dwight said, 'If they're gonna pay for it, let's give it a shot.' And it was completely goofy. Some of the stuff is pretty cool, but it's just a sidebar."

Though the inclusion of some previously released material tagged it as a compilation, it has few hits, and none that would be a sales hook for the anti-Nashville European maverick music crowd. But it's more cohesive than *If There Was a Way*, combining four of the songs from that album that strayed furthest from country formula, with a selection of covers that suggested an appreciation for radio rock that extended well beyond honky-tonk traditionalism.

Beginning with "Things We Said Today," one of the more underappreciated minor-key masterpieces in the Beatles' canon, the album continues with the Grateful Dead's "Truckin'," "Here Comes the Night" by Van Morrison's Them, and another Elvis Presley classic—"Suspicious Minds"—that would soon be bringing Dwight's live performances to an extended, show-stopping climax.

But the real sleeper here is "Hey Little Girl," a 1966 garageband nugget by the Syndicate of Sound, representing yet another slice of California's musical legacy. Yoakam's spokenword sneer absolutely nails the song's pitiless putdown of a girl who played around and paid the price. The glory years of one-hit-wonder AM radio had shaped Yoakam's sensibility, as a performance like this clearly attests. The collection once again gives a prized spot to "Long White Cadillac," making it the emphatic closer to an album that refused to submit to the yardstick of honky-tonk authenticity. And yet remained quintessentially Dwight Yoakam.

13

Wild Ride

ALONG THE WALL OF the conference room of Yoakam's business office on West Hollywood's Sunset Boulevard, punctuating that panoramic view that underscores success, is a series of framed commemorative albums, gold and platinum, the kind so prized throughout the recording industry. They proceed chronologically, from left to right, serving as signposts to Yoakam's commercial trajectory. (As stated before, gold indicates sales of half a million units; platinum is sales of a million.) *Guitars, Cadillacs, Etc., Etc.*: double platinum. *Hillbilly Deluxe*: platinum. *Buenas Noches from a Lonely Room*: gold. *If There Was a Way*: gold.

And then, *This Time*: triple platinum.

Released in March 1993, two and a half years after Yoakam's previous recording of new material, the album found the artist and producer Pete Anderson shooting for the moon. And hitting it. Even though, by Yoakam's categorization, this would be the second album in his second trilogy, it seems more like a brand new chapter, a major leap. It was not only an album where the material was all recently composed—rather than drawn from the backlog, re-recorded from the demo, powered by the muscle memory of years of live performance—but it was the first of Yoakam's albums to employ the recording studio as a creative instrument, even a magician's lab, to extend his artistic vistas much farther than he had ever done on the bandstand.

According to Pete Anderson, the album fulfilled an artistic mission that had begun with *If There Was a Way*, to take Dwight's music to a category beyond country, where his artistry would be recognized as sui generis.

"I wanted to get to a point where we made *Dwight Yoakam music*," he explains. "First off, we made country music. We were bound by the constraints of making a good country record, so you have a fiddle, you have a mandolin, you had certain stuff to choose from. But whatever Johnny Cash was, Johnny Cash made Johnny Cash music. Was it country, was it folk, was it Americana, was it rockabilly? It was Johnny Cash music.

"And Kenny Rogers, for better or worse, made Kenny Rogers music. I wanted Dwight to be in that stratosphere. Ray Charles, all these guys that just made their own kind of music. They did what they wanted, and, eventually, 'Ah, this is Ray Charles.' And we wanted it to be, 'Ah, that's Dwight Yoakam.'"

Whatever chances Dwight had previously taken, his artistry had generally been anchored in a specific place and time—the classic honky-tonk of the mid-twentieth century. Here, in the hit that would become one of Dwight's redefining signature tunes, he was floating above the earth, unmoored, as if in the suspended animation of a dream: "I'm a thousand miles from nowhere," he croons languidly. "Time don't matter to me." With a soaring double-tracked guitar coda (as if

Anderson were channeling both Eric Clapton and Duane All-man), the song rocketed toward the top of the country charts despite sounding nothing like country music and nothing like anything Yoakam had previously recorded. Instead, it evoked a surrealistic twist on Ricky Nelson's "Travelin' Man," filtered through Chris Isaak, exploding into Derek and the Dominos, for a film by David Lynch. As Dwight put it in his memorable chorus hook, "Oh I . . . Oh, I . . . Oh, I . . . Oh, aye-aye-aye-aye-aye-aye-aye-uh-aye."

The album found Yoakam hitting his artistic and commercial peak at a time when the artist and country music were at a crossroads. Yoakam and Anderson spent more time and money on this than on any of his previous releases, and they had no intention of squandering those resources on an experimental vanity project. Four of the tracks renewed his collaborative songwriting relationship with country hitmaker Kostas (who also shared songwriting credit on a fifth track). Now that Yoakam had established such a consistent commercial track record, songwriters figured that working with him or placing a song with him promised a ticket to platinum royalties.

Among those Yoakam-Kostas collaborations was the title track, which hewed closely to the sound and phrasing of a Buck Owens classic. Even so, Dwight would introduce the song on his tour in support of the album as "kind of a psychobilly thing," showing that he was thinking well outside the box of conventional categorization, without forsaking the sort of songcraft that would sustain his legitimacy as a contemporary country hitmaker.

"I think that was an attempt to ensure that they had some radio-friendly stuff," says Dusty Wakeman of the collaborations with Kostas on the album that credited Wakeman as "associate producer" for the first time. While solidifying his country base, Dwight was in full flight creatively.

"Dwight was already a star and the budgets got a lot bigger and nobody was in a rush," continues Wakeman. "We had time to experiment. That was kind of like our *Sgt. Pepper* period. And that was a lot of fun."

Too many successful artists, particularly country artists, don't exercise such freedom. Success more often becomes a prison of expectations rather than a liberation from formula. There's a pressure to repeat whatever has proven so popular in the past. Particularly amid the aftershocks of Garth, the raising of the commercial stakes turned some hit acts (and those who aspired to be) even more conservative, succumbing to the pressure not only to give their audience what it wanted, but to give *Garth's* audience what *it* wanted.

The decade thus spawned countless mini-Garths, so-called "hat acts," artists with the right look and sound to appeal to the largest audience that country music had ever known, but without the emotional depth or the working-class roots that had long defined the best country music. Garth was a commercial juggernaut, but Dwight Yoakam was a visionary artist, as he confirmed with *This Time*. And, without forsaking the country market, he was aiming for a wider world.

That wider world responded with greater recognition for Dwight than he had ever received before. Amid the new math of commerce A.G., *This Time* didn't top the country charts, as Yoakam's early albums routinely had, settling instead in the top five. Yet sales spurred it into the top twenty-five of the pop charts as well (the first time that he'd cracked the Top 50 on the pop side of the street). And *Rolling Stone*, which had previously paid scant attention to contemporary commercial country, not only raved about the album in a four-star review, but accorded it the prestige position of the long lead review.

That piece, in the June 10, 1993, issue, is headlined "The Time Has Come for Dwight" and bylined by me. I had moved at the start of the decade from Chicago to Austin, drawn in some measure by the hothouse insurgence of music that fused country tradition with rock attitude but never settled into anything so tepid as "country rock." In Austin, I found so many artists who were trying to do what Yoakam was, though none would enjoy anything close to his commercial success. Though I'd written about everything from punk rock to free jazz and beyond during my decade at the *Chicago Sun-Times*, I inevitably became pegged as the "Austin guy" after the move, frequently assigned to write about roots music for a variety of national publications.

One of my earliest benefactors was Anthony DeCurtis, then editor of the reviews section for *Rolling Stone*. I'd begun working for Anthony while still in Chicago, but it was after my move that he proposed I write an occasional column, every couple of months, as a roots music roundup under the banner "Country & Western." The initiative reflected a recognition that there was something happening here at the juncture of country and rock that had reached critical mass, but that the most inspired music in this amorphous category was flying under the radar of Nashville.

In fact, the very title of the "Country & Western" column was considered an anachronism by the Nashville recording industry, if not downright insulting. Commercial country had spent decades trying to distance itself from the raw, rough "western" side of its heritage, and here was a column rubbing its nose in it. (Like Yoakam and his ilk had with "hillbilly.") One leading Nashville publicist suggested that this was akin to launching a column on contemporary R&B and calling it "Race Records."

From *Rolling Stone*'s standpoint, decisions on what to cover, both in the column and in the larger reviews section, would be made according to musical significance rather than commercial country success. And such coverage would be designed to appeal to the magazine's core readership—fans of rock, popular music, and pop culture in general—rather than the self-indentified (albeit growing) fan base of mainstream country. So, yes, *Rolling Stone* would acknowledge country music, but not necessarily in the way Nashville wanted it to. (The Garth Brooks cover story would come later.)

That lead review for Dwight reinforced the difference. "When Dwight Yoakam hoisted the 'hillbilly music' banner in the mid-eighties," I wrote, "the country establishment reacted with the sort of enthusiasm usually reserved for flatulence in church. As country music was homogenizing itself to win soft-rock suburbia, it wanted no reminders of its raw rural past.

"Yoakam's voice was too nasal, his subject matter too honky-tonk, his jeans too tight. Uncompromising and defiant, he sang with the conviction of a fundamentalist who felt that he was following the one true path—and that the rest of country music had gone astray."

After introducing Yoakam to rock fans who perhaps had previously paid scant or no attention, and providing context as to his accomplishment, the review proceeded to celebrate "the finest showcase to date of Yoakam's artistry, one that downplays the anti-hero aura to focus attention on what is best in the singer and his songs . . . That he no longer sounds like an artist with something to prove represents stronger proof than ever of his artistry."

For Yoakam, artistic growth required letting go, or at least loosening his grip. At the heart of *This Time* lies an aesthetic contradiction, one that makes him such a vital, provocative, occasionally confounding artist. For Yoakam had established his identity as the purest of honky-tonk purists (though honky-tonk "purity," like "authenticity," is itself a quality rife with contradiction; it exists in the ear of the beholder). And here he was positioning himself not merely "a thousand miles from no-where," but a couple thousand from the nearest honky-tonk.

"This was one of the more experimental songs Dwight has written," explained Pete Anderson of "Thousand Miles" in a track-by-track analysis for the *Journal of Country Music* (Vol. 15, No. 3). "There's a long guitar outro, a la 'Layla.' The song has a grand epic sound because it was originally inspired by and written for a movie (*Red Rock West*), although the film producers would not pay for it to be remixed for Sensurround, so we didn't let them do it."

Anderson says that the biggest decision concerning the track was "putting this song on a Dwight album at all." Though this risky move paid dividends for Yoakam, with "A Thousand Miles From Nowhere" ranking with his most successful and beloved country hits, it wasn't close to country in the way that Yoakam and fans had previously defined the term. It certainly wasn't rock. Perhaps it was pop, most expansively defined. But mostly it served notice that music this rapturously gorgeous required neither categorization nor justification.

"Oftentimes we're not doing country music anymore," Dwight admitted to Steve Pond in the May 1993, issue of *Us* magazine (*Rolling Stone*'s sister publication, celeb-oriented and general interest like *People*). "But that's okay. Country music is not where I'll always remain, but it's a place that I'll always return to."

The magazine proclaimed "This Time, Dwight Yoakam Unleashes the Album of His Life," and the artist tended to agree, saying that it was "truly, totally my voice." He continued, "It's been a musical journey for me, and this is the most *mapless* leg of the journey so far."

The journey begins with one of the kitschiest arrangements in Yoakam's repertoire, with "Pocket of a Clown" returning to the sort of countrypolitan backing chorus that he and

Anderson had employed to such surprising (at the time) effect five years earlier on "Always Late with Your Kisses." But where that cover took its seal of credibility from the Lefty Frizzell songbook, "Pocket of a Clown" sounds more conceptually daring, as if Dwight is working without a net, the lyrics combining a surrealistic visual image with a chorus hook that borders on haiku in its elliptical simplicity: "Hollow lies make a thin disguise as little drops of truth fall from your eyes."

Having prepped the audience for something new with the album opener, Yoakam and Anderson threw the musical road map out the window with "A Thousand Miles from Nowhere," the second cut. From there, he had the freedom to go anywhere, and he did.

"Ain't That Lonely Yet" even employs strings by Paul Buckmaster, best known for his work with noted honky cat Elton John. Orchestral arrangements in any sort of popular music are often referred to as "sweetening," but there's nothing sweet about a song that would be hailed as another Dwight classic, with its beguiling, languid melody beneath a kiss-off lyric as deceptive as Bob Dylan's "Don't Think Twice, It's All Right."

It's noteworthy that nowhere on the album did Yoakam travel into territory that could be classified as "country rock." Instead, there are stone-cold country cuts here—"Home for Sale," "Two Doors Down," "King of Fools," the closing "Lonesome Roads"—that are as timeless and tradition-bound as Yoakam's brand of country music gets.

Such performances feature Yoakam's most nuanced and masterful vocals to date, confirming that, as my *Rolling Stone* rave put it, "The man can flat-out sing . . . Though Yoakam is rarely mentioned with Randy Travis or John Anderson among the first rank of neo-traditionalist vocal virtuosos, *This Time* suggests that he has no contemporary peer, that his emotional precision and command of nuance have attained a kind of perfection—if you can imagine Buck Owens and Johnny Horton as spiritual mentors."

He distills that perfection into one twisted phrase, in "Two Doors Down," another of his drown-your-heartbreak-in-alcohol honky-tonk reveries. "Freedom from sorrow," sings the hopeful vocalist, "is just two doors away," as "two doors" somehow extends itself into more syllables than even George Jones might have thought possible. As the devout abstainer sings again about getting drunk, country vocals don't get any more convincing and emotionally compelling than this.

At the other polarity of the album's musical dynamic, the rock numbers pull out all the stops, rocking with a swagger beyond anything he'd previously written, matching the intensity of "Long White Cadillac" and upping the ante. It's certainly not rockabilly or even punk rock, let alone country rock. It carries barely a whiff of dusty anachronism, though you can hear in "Fast As You" an emulation of the driving, pulsating sensuality that Roy Orbison had brought to "Oh, Pretty Woman."

"'Fast As You' was an intelligent lyric written to an uptempo groove, which is a pretty lethal combination," says producer Anderson. "Wow! That was a big rocket ship for that record. And then 'A Thousand Miles From Nowhere,' that was one song where I felt I really needed to dig in, guitar-wise. Cause the chord changes were nothing that special, but the lyric was beautiful, and the melody was beautiful. So I'm very proud of that, and we had some groundbreaking stuff for both of us, as artists.

"And as a producer, I did the record in Pro Tools, which was in its infancy. And it's a massive record, a big, ass-kicking record. 'Pocket of a Clown' was another 'What the . . . ?' These aren't your cousin Homer writing from behind the barn.

There's some thoughts going into this stuff, some twists and turns that you don't expect, and then the music was definitely up to snuff."

"Fast As You" didn't sound nearly as country as its flip side on the single ("Home for Sale") or the earlier single that it followed (the lush, bittersweet "Try Not to Look So Pretty"), but it proved a huge hit for Yoakam on country radio and a calling card for rock appeal. Plainly, Yoakam's hard-core country following was not only allowing him to stretch himself, it was encouraging him to do so, and rewarding him for it.

"Wild Ride" evokes the Rolling Stones, and not the country-ish "No Expectations"/"Wild Horses" side of the Stones, but the "Tumblin' Dice" side, loose and edgy and sexy. Not a hit and never intended to be, it nonetheless provides the album with both an anthem and a theme. "Are you ready for the wild ride?" the song asks the singer, who in turn asks his audience. The response would prove resoundingly affirmative.

The album's sequencing corresponds to Yoakam's quote concerning country music as the place where he'll always return. Following "Wild Ride," the concluding "Lonesome Road" is quintessential Yoakam country—a lachrymose ballad that is almost a parody of self-pity, a song that one could imagine Hank Williams performing (though "I'm So Lonesome I Could Cry" sounds positively chipper in comparison).

"Lonesome roads are the only kind I ever travel," sings Dwight. "Empty rooms are the only place I ever stay. I'm just a face out in the crowd that looks like trouble. Poor ol' worthless me is the only friend I ever made."

While we ponder the unclear reference (is it the face or the crowd that "looks like trouble"? Or both?), let's agree with Yoakam that no matter how far afield he has traveled on this mapless musical journey, he hasn't betrayed his vision of country music, but extended it. He has reinforced his identity as a country artist while expanding the possibility of what a country artist could be.

That such an album could be a favorite among fans who considered their primary musical allegiance to be country, critics who celebrated the music's significance in the wider world of popular culture (and were often suspicious of commercial country), and initiates who were discovering that even if you didn't like country music or the state it currently found itself, you might just like Dwight, attests again to the singularity of the artist's musical achievement.

It isn't that often that all the stars align, that critical response, commercial success, and the artist's own view of his peak coincide. With *This Time*, Dwight scaled the summit, as the album was hailed as the high point of his career then and has become more uniformly recognized as such with the passage of time.

YOAKAM FOLLOWED THE most ambitious album of his career with his most ambitious tour to date, one that took him beyond the clubs and concert halls to the arenas of the nation. And where he showed that he could project his music to fifteen thousand or so delirious fans with the same power and intensity that he had once flashed to hundreds from a club bandstand. On the boisterous *Dwight Live*, recorded at the comparatively intimate (for this tour) Warfield Theatre in San Francisco, Yoakam acknowledges everyone who had helped make *This Time* such a success, and anybody who had ever bought any of his albums, because "you've allowed me to make a living doing what I did for a long time for free. And I thank you for that."

Most live country albums stick pretty close to recorded arrangements of the hits, or as close as the touring band can come to the musicianship of the Nashville studio A-listers.

(Even the most successful country stars rarely take their touring musicians into a Nashville studio; Dwight has always recorded with his live band.) Many sound as if they had simply dubbed in some applause. Dwight's is a live album in more of a rock sense, feeding off the audience's response, which seems to send a charge through the band and amp up the energy of the interplay. It's the sort of live album the Rolling Stones have made.

Where *This Time* was definitely a studio creation, going well beyond the dynamic of the bandstand performance captured on Yoakam's earlier albums, *Dwight Live* pulls no punches as it strips the material of its studio polish. It also leaves no doubts about the scope of his ambition. The album opens with an Elvis Presley hit—"Little Sister"—and crescendos to a climax with a more recent Elvis Presley hit, the concluding "Suspicious Minds," with more than half of the seven-minute performance an instrumental outro that whips the crowd into a multi-orgasmic frenzy. Even when Dwight isn't singing Elvis, he might imitate him (as on the mumbling phrasing of "It Only Hurts When I Cry").

The album spotlights Anderson's guitar as much as Yoakam's vocals, with the lead instrument filling what were the wide open spaces of "A Thousand Miles from Nowhere," and putting the pedal to the metal on "Fast As You" and "Long White Cadillac." Even "Please, Please Baby" accelerates to a fury beyond its earliest incarnation as a favorite from the punk rock clubs.

It's plain from the performance that Yoakam is no longer playing the rube, as he was when the tape was rolling at the Roxy for that early radio broadcast. Onstage, he isn't talking much at all, beyond offering sincere thanks. But offstage, I would discover, his mouth still operated in overdrive. When his tour came to Austin for a performance at the Frank Erwin

Center—the basketball arena for the University of Texas Longhorns—his publicist told me that Yoakam would like me to come to his tour bus so he could say hi.

I usually avoid anything backstage or offstage, unless in the line of duty (i.e., an interview). But I liked Dwight, hadn't seen him for a few years, and he'd apparently appreciated my review in *Rolling Stone*. At the concert, my wife and I went where the publicist had told me we should at the appointed time and discovered that there was a bunch of folks there to be shuttled in smaller groups to Dwight's bus for the standard industry "meet and greet."

I figured I had my out, and that Dwight would never miss me. Heck, it had probably been the publicist's idea for us to get together. So we went back to our seats, and I thought that was the end of it. Until I went to the office the next morning, checked my voice mail, and discovered I had five messages.

They were all from Dwight, and each ran the generous length that the voice mail system permitted. After which, interrupted, he had immediately called back and picked up where he'd left off, rambling about the review, our earlier encounter in Chicago, how he was hoping his people hadn't screwed up since we hadn't gotten together the previous night . . . It made me sorry that I hadn't made more of an effort to stick it out. But mostly it amazed me with Dwight's stamina and perseverance as a monologist.

It was like we were having a conversation, picking up where we'd left off at the Ritz-Carlton in Chicago, so many years earlier. Only he was the only one talking, for twenty minutes or so, refusing to let a phone system cut him off for good. When I arranged to get together with Dwight for this book, I mentioned this incident to his assistant, who nodded in recognition. "Dwight," she said, "is the king of voice mail messages."

14

Gone, Real Gone

HOW FAR IS TOO FAR? Released after another interval of two and a half years—much of it spent in powerhouse concert performance, as documented in the May 1995 release of *Dwight Live*—Yoakam's next studio album plainly found the artist and his producer encouraged by the reception for *This Time*, which had easily been the most eclectic, ambitious, and conceptually creative album of Yoakam's career. And the best received as well.

So they returned with the aptly titled *Gone*, which pushed the envelope farther in every possible direction, and which confounded all expectations except the one that insisted that, where Yoakam was concerned, you should expect the unexpected. You could call *Gone* the most polarizing album of Yoakam's career, the turning point of his commercial downturn. You could consider it one of his best, certainly his bravest. Or you could simply label it Dwight's WTF??? album.

"That album had this splitting up of our musical atom, so to speak," says Yoakam with a laugh. "With Pete controlling the engineering, and then me throwing paint over my shoulder at times. Like when Lennon walked in with [he starts singing], 'Let me take you down, 'cause I'm going to . . .' That's what we had the freedom to do."

Says Anderson, "I think *Gone* was the best possible record to follow *This Time*. I was aware of that pressure, and I'm extremely proud of that record. And I may get flack from outside the immediate circle, but I think everybody [at the label] dropped the ball on that record. The reviews on that record are incredible. Just read the press kit! It's a beautiful, beautiful record."

Again, a less daring artist might have chosen not to exercise that freedom, preferring to solidify his gains with "Another Thousand Miles From Nowhere" and "Still Ain't That Lonely Yet." Instead Dwight responded with an album that reflects the extent of his creative ambition better than anything else he has ever recorded. After more than a year of immersing myself in the music of Dwight Yoakam, I'm still not sure I'm ready to pronounce it the best album of his career. But it has become my favorite.

"*Gone* was totally like, 'Let's go crazy,' and I knew that going in," says Dusty Wakeman of the last Yoakam album where he would be credited as associate producer. "It's an overlooked gem, but it came at a time when his relationship with Warner Bros. had soured a little bit. It got no airplay. Killer record."

How is it different? Let us count the ways, starting with what seem to be minor matters of packaging and personnel. The coloring of the cover is such that the largest and brightest of the capital letters simply blare "DWIGHT," in a turquoise that is almost neon. Much smaller letters have "GONE" in comparatively subtle white, while the darker blue of "YOAKAM" is almost invisible, until you look really hard in the right light.

Was Dwight becoming a one-name artist (as *Dwight Live* perhaps anticipated)—the Madonna or Cher of contemporary country? Many of the package's photos, which obscure the artist's eyes behind sunglasses or in the shadow of his white hat's brim, look like stills from an update of *Midnight Cowboy*. There's also a piece of art in the booklet, an abstract oil by Hans Burkhardt, an expressionist well known in art circles but not exactly a household name among the honky-tonk crowd.

Are you sure Garth done it this a-way?

The album also marked the replacement of drummer Jeff Donavan, the last of the original Babylonian Cowboys recruited by Anderson, with Jim Christie, who had played with the band on the extended tour for *This Time*. (Donavan has continued to work with Anderson, drumming on the guitarist's 2011 album, *Even Things Up*.) Another surprise found background vocals on two cuts supplied by the Rembrandts, pop-rock lightweights whose "I'll Be There for You" remains in power rotation in TV reruns as the theme song for *Friends*.

But the music itself relegates such credit changes to the margins of ephemera. Whatever strictures of tradition Yoakam's music had followed throughout his career, he spent most of *Gone* subverting them, exploding them, transcending them. He served notice with the mariachi-laced "Sorry You Asked?" opener that this would be a different Dwight, one whose deadpan sense of the absurd was in full force, one who refused to be limited either by audience expectations or by the artistic identity he'd established through his previous success.

The song is a glorious goof, a Marty Robbins ballad set to a Johnny Cash rhythm, fueled by the alcohol that Yoakam never drank. Imagine settling down on a barstool, ordering a beer, and asking the guy next to you how he's doing. And then listening as he responds by going on . . . and on . . . and on . . . until it's apparent that the story will continue even after you've left. Maybe even after the bar has closed. (As the song fades, the singer and his narrative are still going strong, picking up steam.)

It's like the Oprah version of an Old West gunfighter ballad, in which the singer who has learned that he must get in touch with his feelings rambles, "I mighta, shoulda seen that we were drifting apart, but I was in what I guess you'd call denial." Or, a verse later, "Okay, we both have the tendency to overreact, so I can't really tell you who's at fault. But there were certain third parties, well her sister for one, who helped bring our reconciling to a drop-dead halt."

It's plain that this episode is building to a Warren Zevon climax (one involving some combination of lawyers, guns, and money), but that won't happen until long after he has exhausted the listener's patience (and Anderson has run out of tape).

From here it was obvious that with *Gone*, anything goes. The album shows Yoakam lightening up and loosening up. The next cut has Dwight turning to the lilt of Buddy Holly for the last thing one would have ever anticipated from Yoakam, a pure love song—in fact a ringing tribute to "the power of love." Listen closely, and you might hear something a little creepy hovering (like the stalker in the Police's "Every Breath You Take"), but by Yoakam's standards this song is lollipops and roses.

If Yoakam sounds uncharacteristically chipper on "Near You," and positively loopy on "Sorry You Asked?" and "Baby Why Not" (another nod toward Texas, with the Sir Douglas Quintet joining Buddy Holly as a source of inspiration), the dark nights of the album's soul are darker and deeper than ever. The titles alone suggest the spiritual abyss of "Nothing" and "Heart of Stone" (the two co-writes with Kostas on an album otherwise composed by Yoakam alone).

"Nothing" shares something of its spirit of reverie with "A Thousand Miles from Nowhere," but this is a much bleaker vision. With its full-bodied organ and call-and-response back-ing chorus, the arrangement owes more to Memphis (and, in particular, Willie Mitchell's work with Al Green) than it does to Nashville, while the taut lyric conveys the pain of loss with-out a hint of redemption. "Nothing but sorrow, nothing but pain, nothing but memories that whisper your name," sings Yoakam in one of his most chilling vocal performances. "Noth-ing but sadness, nothing but fear, nothing but silence is heard around here."

"Heart of Stone" sounds more like classic country (to which, as Yoakam insisted around the release of *This Time*, he'd always return), closing the album with a cowboy lope and a Jordanaires-style backing vocal, with an indelible lyric set to a memorable melody. There's an irony in the perspective, as the singer makes plain that he isn't as stone-hearted as he might pretend to be, that "This heart of stone sure is missing you, sure is wishing you were back where love belongs."

In retrospect, it sounds like it could have been, should have been, another one of Yoakam's signature hit singles. Yet it was never released to country radio as a single, and those cuts that were—the soulful "Nothing" and the up-tempo title cut—didn't enjoy nearly the success that Yoakam routinely had for the previous decade.

The strains between the Los Angeles–based artist and the Nashville-based country industry didn't seem so significant as long as both sides were benefitting commercially. But with *Gone*, the tensions would intensify, with the contention over whether Yoakam had refused to give his Nashville label some-thing it could sell, or whether the label hadn't been able to suc-cessfully promote music that radio resisted from an artist that the country industry considered increasingly difficult.

"Truthfully, I think a combination of things happened be-hind the scenes," says Anderson. "Not in a conspiratorial way, it's just the nature of the business. And we just didn't get the hammer that we needed. It's a great, great record, and it's a shame what happened to it. Not to cast aspersions on Jim Ed Norman (then head of Warner Bros. Nashville), because he was a big, big guy for me, but I don't know how anybody could not put the hammer down. Like, 'I'm not taking no for an answer from radio. Forget it.' And if we'd had that one on top of *This Time*, who knows what would have happened?"

If Jim Ed knows, he isn't telling. Never have I encountered someone who declined to be interviewed as graciously, eloquently, warmly, humorously—or at such length—as Jim Ed Norman. When I called him for comment, he provided so much context on the music industry, the essence of radio, the relationship between art and commerce, that he convinced me that his inclusion would require a chapter or more all its own. Or maybe Norman should write his own book, a project he has been threatening through thirty-five years of dealing with the media (with the working title of *Yeah, That's What I Said, But It's Not What I Meant!*)

So he made a convincing case that any response he made, stripped of context, would be perceived as a sound bite rebuttal to Pete—ancient history that would benefit no one at this point. "Dwight is an amazing creator, performer, and artist," says the record exec whom both artist and producer credit with giving them creative autonomy and crucial support. "And Pete is an amazing producer—the sound he created is extraordinary, and the work they did together was extraordinary. This book isn't about Warner Bros. or the vagaries of the music business at the time, and you've got a great subject whether Jim Ed participates or not."

Fair enough. But I asked Norman if I could quote him on artists and labels in general, on the contention that label commitment determines the commercial fate of the music. Here's a very small part of what he explained: "Some of the things you do as an artist resonate with the public. And, I'm sorry, but some of the things that you do, don't. And you know what? It's no different for the biggest successes in the history of the industry.

"Radio is in the advertising business. We go through periods where radio plays the music no one hates, rather than the music people love. Their approach is don't play music that has a high tune-out quotient, because they need to keep people listening to their station. If they don't, it affects how much they can charge for advertising. And there's never been an artist who has escaped radio being less enthusiastic today than they were yesterday for their efforts." (He also made a very funny reference to "Maxwell's Silver Hammer.")

Wherever the fault lies, in the product or with the label, the airwaves or the gods—and this isn't an either/or proposition—*Gone* marked the end of Dwight's days as a consistent country hitmaker. Yet Yoakam benefitted in the wider world from more publicity than he had previously received, in-depth feature profiles in particular. If *This Time* had taken some by surprise—showing the full dimensions of an artist caricatured as a honky-tonk throwback or a latter-day Buckaroo—the press was ready for him with *Gone*. And Dwight, never reluctant to talk, confirmed that he was an artist quite unlike any that country music had previously seen.

As he explained in an eight-page cover spread for *New Country* ("A Thousand Miles from Nowhere," November 1995), "History repeats itself, but at an accelerated pace, and that's why we miss a lot of it—we're a microcosm now of this past empire or republic. So the only thing certain in the universe is movement. That's all we're referring to when we talk about time, the calibration of movement. Earth around the sun, moon around the Earth, the sun through its galaxy and on out through the universe.

"It's just movement, and it's as if the universe is on this massive journey. From where and to where, I don't know, but we're all part of that journey, and if we feel that things are accelerating, I think that's just the nature of existence. Now it may implode on itself sometimes, may collapse, but maybe *that* is the natural progression of existence, and I don't think it's a downer. I would give over to it, not fight with it so much?"

So what can a poor boy do, except to sing for a honky-tonk band? And maybe peer through the telescope pointed out the window of his West Hollywood office.

"I don't think I've come up with anything besides the work," he said in the same exhaustive profile. "But perhaps the work is its own justification, because I don't look at it as work. I don't want to be frightfully over-romantic about it, but it's kinda what I do. It's what I did when I was not getting paid for it, and what I did when I was a kid. I always wanted to stand there and make this noise."

Or, as he explained of his music to frequent interviewer Patrick Carr, for a profile in *Country Music* ("Semantics & Style," November–December 1995), "It's a melting pot . . . I don't think I'll ever be able to escape that. I think it'll become more and more that. The first three albums were probably my need to express the cornerstones, my foundation musically and the things I first heard from my parents growing up in Ohio, the things they brought with them from Kentucky, the things that I still use as a primary foundation for what I do musically, but beyond that . . ."

(Let's pause here. Just try to read that last sentence aloud— recognizing that it isn't even a complete sentence—without stopping at least once for a deep breath.)

". . . Pete and I have talked about it, that I come from that time when music just exploded on AM radio. You would hear Buck Owens come right behind the Beatles or the Stones and lead them into Van Morrison, and then go into maybe the

Statler Brothers doing 'Flowers in the Wall,' Henson Cargill doing 'Skip a Rope.' All that stuff. King Curtis, of course, the 'Soul Twist' stuff, and Booker T. and the MG's, Otis Redding, the Box Tops; that Motown thing exploded. Motown, too. From '63 to '67 Motown was all over the place. *Everything* was going on."

There are times when I think that Dwight Yoakam and Tom Petty are musical brothers, kindred spirits who happen to find themselves on opposite sides of the categorical tracks. Both are deeply steeped in the eclecticism of '60s AM radio. Both are very intelligent and intuitive Southern guys who feel an affinity for a white-trash sensibility (and perhaps have a chip on the shoulder reflecting that). Both owe a deep debt to the music of the Byrds (as the jangle of early Petty attests on hits like "American Girl"). Both have high foreheads and similar builds. They even look a little alike.

"I get stopped occasionally from people who think I'm him," says Yoakam when I mention the comparison. "I don't know if he gets that about me. I've always dug his whole thing with the jangly, Byrds-style guitar. One of the songs of his I thought of covering years ago was [searches for the right key, tunes again, starts singing], 'You think you're gonna take her away, with your money and your cocaine.'"

Though Yoakam never has gotten around to covering "Listen to Her Heart"—which he absolutely nailed, from memory, for me—"Never Hold You" on *Gone* would fit just fine on a Petty album, a hopped-up cousin of "Don't Come Around Here No More," with a guitar figure from Anderson straight from the AM '60s of "Over Under Sideways Down" by the Yardbirds (another favorite Petty band, whose version of "I'm a Man" he's long covered in concert).

As Anderson explains, perhaps one of the reasons that *Gone* sounds significantly different from any Yoakam album that had come before, or would come after, is that Dwight wrote these songs differently, on electric guitar rather than his usual acoustic.

"He was really getting into electric guitar then, and he had a different one in every room of his house," says Pete. "After that, I'm glad he got away from it, because I think his strength is writing on an acoustic. But he came up with ideas, because just strumming the different guitars puts you into a different frame. So he was really flexing his muscles. And he was learning the tricks."

Reinforcing the melting-pot motif, "One More Night" is a soul-shuddering ballad that features both a Stax/Volt horn chart and a lead sitar from Anderson. Which might seem all the more peculiar until you recall Joe South's use of the instrument on "Games People Play," a recording that we'd now call country but then knew as a '60s AM smash. (South would also make crucial contributions to Bob Dylan's *Blonde on Blonde*, recorded in Nashville, at a time in the mid-1960s when so much seemed up for grabs.)

As the country music critic for Nashville's *Tennessean* (the journalistic equivalent of covering the automobile industry for a Detroit paper, or the film industry as a Hollywood journalist), Robert K. Oermann put Yoakam's achievement into country-music perspective:

"Yoakam's new *Gone* CD comes in the wake of 1993's *This Time*, the biggest-selling album of his career. Instead of duplicating the earlier effort, the California maverick has smashed all musical borders and concocted a brew of startling diversity and originality.

"Tom-toms pulse beneath his voice, strings sigh, an organ hums darkly, horns punctuate the mix. Is that an Indian sitar we hear? Bongos, Mexicali trumpets, and electric guitars swirl through the album, creating hypnotic sonic textures. Riding above it all is the unmistakable hillbilly drawl of a man who has made a career of defying expectations."

In retrospect, *Gone* represents the point where his career went south—in terms of commercial country hits, that is. His music would never again scale the heights of country success that it previously had done routinely. *Gone* found Yoakam generating more publicity than ever, but *This Time* remains celebrated as his creative and commercial peak, the album where he put it all together. Which makes *Gone*, in comparison, the album where he threw it all away.

"I was truly disappointed in the lack of success of *Gone*," says Anderson. "And it wasn't a slow decline. We went from a triple platinum record to a record that sold three hundred and fifty thousand copies. And then sold more through record clubs than it did at retail. What does that tell you? It tells me people didn't even know the record was out."

Even if it reached more people through record clubs— those "buy ten records for a penny" deals that once stocked the music library of the Yoakam household—the daring brilliance of *Gone* remains its own reward. None of the principals who worked on it consider it anything like a mistake or a failure; all are proud of its achievement more than fifteen years later. No one was suffering from the delusion that "startling originality" was a sure bet for country acceptance.

Whatever the album's commercial fate, Yoakam had other fish to fry. He'd been interested in acting even longer than he'd been performing music, and he'd been amusing himself with bit parts in interesting flicks such as *Red Rock West*. Yet he was making a greater commitment to this sidelight with a key role in a film by his buddy (and sometimes fellow musician) Billy Bob Thornton, a forthcoming movie that every profile timed to the release of *Gone* referenced as *Some Folks Call It a Slingblade*.

Released the following year as *Sling Blade*, the film would establish Yoakam's credibility as an actor (one who was willing to play a really bad guy and even take off his hat!) and would profoundly affect his career trajectory. It also earned Billy Bob

Thornton a screenplay Oscar and a best actor nomination, with the whole cast recognized with a Screen Actors Guild nomination for best ensemble acting.

Yoakam insists that making movies never compromised his focus on music or provided a distraction. But it did give him other options beyond touring and making albums. And there's no question that it would ultimately put a strain on his working relationship with Pete Anderson.

15

Act Naturally

THIS IS A BOOK ABOUT Dwight Yoakam's music. It is tangentially about the music business. It is barely about his private life: his loves, his friends, his outside interests. But it necessarily must touch upon his movie career, for a couple of different reasons. One is that the more serious Dwight became about acting in particular and making movies in general, the less he focused his artistry exclusively on music. He remained a musical artist with an acting alternative, but there were times when he seemed more intrigued by the alternative than by his bread-and-butter career.

The second reason is that some—particularly some who are critical of Dwight—insist that these aren't two separate creative outlets at all. They are the ones who dismiss Dwight as a poseur who had been acting the part of a honky-tonk traditionalist from the start of his career.

When I was talking to one veteran musician who had been part of the same SoCal roots-country scene as Dwight, and asked in passing if he had anything to say about Yoakam, he said he didn't. This was a surprisingly common response from those who hadn't worked directly with Dwight, and even from some who had worked closely with him decades ago, and seemed to reflect the advice I'd heard long ago from my mother: "If you can't say anything nice, don't say anything at all."

But then the musician offered, deadpan, "He's a pretty good actor." And I don't think he was referring to the movies. Or at least not exclusively.

Let's remember that it was acting that led Yoakam into performing music in the first place, that it was his high school theater background that gave him the confidence to assume the role of lead singer in a Sha Na Na–type band for his school's talent show. And that the reaction he generated changed the course of his life. But even after he arrived in Southern California, he took a role in a community stage production before he formed a band and began playing the honky-tonks.

In one of the first "local boy makes good" profiles back home, in the Sunday magazine for Louisville's *Courier-Journal* ("Hot Honky-Tonk," August 3, 1986), Dwight's younger brother David told reporter Ronni Lundy, "Drama was a big thing for him. He's been a ham all his life. When he was little, about in second grade, we'd come home from church, and the other kids would change into play clothes. Here would come Dwight with his little bow tie on, just like he was onstage."

And whether others meant it as dismissal, a sign of his lack of authenticity, Dwight showed early on that he *is* a good actor, and an ambitious one, for all the right reasons. His acting ambitions and range extend well beyond playing a version of his musical persona in order to cross-promote his celebrity. He's had twenty-five roles since his 1993 debut in *Red Rock*

West, but the one that really opened eyes was the redneck loudmouth Doyle Hargraves in 1996's *Sling Blade*, the breakthrough for Dwight's buddy, fellow actor-musician Billy Bob Thornton.

Balding, evil, and decidedly unromantic, Doyle showcased a whole different side of Dwight than the honky-tonk heartthrob his fans had embraced. And critics and movie fans who might only have been dimly aware of Yoakam's brand of country music took favorable notice of his performance. One critic who had plainly been aware of Dwight was Janet Maslin, who had written mainly about rock before becoming a film critic (and now a book critic) for the *New York Times*, and whose *Sling Blade* review praised Dwight's "strong, solid" acting as "the teasingly malevolent Doyle."

For purely commercial reasons, Pete Anderson didn't see much benefit in Dwight's choice of roles. "If that was his sidebar, what he wanted to do, fine," he says. "I was initially hoping, just from the perspective of a producer who had points [a percentage of profits] on the record, that it could really help record sales. But he was pretty bent on not being himself in a movie or taking advantage of that. He wanted to truly be an actor and disguise himself in a part, as opposed to, 'Why don't you do a singing cowboy movie? And we'll do a soundtrack and sell more records!'"

So Dwight's acting career became a whole separate thing, one in which he eagerly submitted to character parts that forced him to stretch rather than higher profile productions in which he could play a version of the guy fans knew from his music videos. And he resisted any suggestion that his work on the film soundstage and on the concert stage had much in common, that each found him playing a role.

"No, I'm not different," says Yoakam, responding to a question about any difference between Dwight offstage and his persona (the role he plays?) on the concert stage. "The context is different. It's like the difference between sitting down and playing the acoustic guitar in concert and then standing up and performing is like the difference between throwing the long pass and when you bootleg or hand off. If it's a short route, I'm already looking to throw it by the second step. But if it's a post route, I don't look for it until I'm four steps back. To use the analogy of sports, because it's a physical thing that we're talking about. It's a physical performance.

"And like you, you have to be different when you lecture," he continues (since we've discussed how my main job these days is teaching journalism). "You're not different; your approach to delivering information is different, based on the necessity of context, environment. I have to capture your attention from the stage. It's not like a record where you open it, take it out, put it on, and play. You're intent on listening. If the kids pick up a book you wrote on a subject, you don't have to contextualize it the same way you would in a lecture. You're imparting information in a different context. So no—I'm not different, context is different."

Point taken. When he's onstage, Dwight isn't *playing* Dwight, Dwight *is* Dwight. At least according to Dwight. For Yoakam, making music is an entirely different occupation from making movies, where his job is to play someone else, often someone very different than Dwight. And both Yoakam and Anderson maintain that, initially at least, the acting detour had no detrimental effect on the musical career. Even with a full career of recording and touring, Yoakam had some down time. And if he chose to spend that down time as an actor, so be it.

Yet *Sling Blade* was released the year after the disappointing commercial reception to *Gone*, the first of Dwight's albums that had tanked, at least in comparison with expectations.

Country music was increasingly becoming a younger person's game, and Dwight wasn't getting any younger. In the wake of Garth and the new generation that followed, you could no longer grow old on commercial country radio, but you could age gracefully as a character actor.

However, a career as a character actor not only shifted the primary focus from music, it left no room for Pete. And not to get ahead of our story, but the more time (and, eventually, money) Dwight invested in a film career, the less he would think of himself exclusively as a musical artist, particularly as it became apparent that he wasn't likely to enjoy the consistent commercial success post-*Gone* that he had from the start of his recording career.

In a 2003 interview with About.com before his split with Yoakam, Anderson seemed both frustrated and mystified by his longtime partner's acting-career detour, responding to a question from Kathy Coleman this way: "My only, I don't know if it's a frustration, but . . . Dwight has, still has and has had the potential to be, you know, the most important country artist of his time," said Anderson. "And that's my personal opinion, and why he would leave, or descend from, or not maintain a mantle of that stature to become a—um, no, I barely, I don't know what kind of—a character actor? A sub-player? You know, he's sort of gotten typecast pretty rapidly as like, kind of a psycho or he plays these mean parts, or hurting people or yelling and screaming and throwing tantrums and shooting and killing and . . . I don't see the movies, I'm not, haven't been attracted to them.

"I saw *Sling Blade*, and I thought *Sling Blade* was okay, I thought the short, the initial short, I thought was really good, the movie was good, but—and Dwight did well in *Sling Blade*, but Dwight sort of . . . Billy Bob, it was a low-budget, low-pressure situation, and I think Billy Bob let Dwight just kinda do his thing, and he was acting, you know, on a lot more casual basis. But, you know, I can't . . . it'd be like somebody saying you know, why do I play so much basketball, I love to play basketball, but I'm not trying to be in the NBA, 'cause that's not gonna happen. I mean, I don't even play in leagues, but it is exercise for me, so maybe it's some sort of exercise for Dwight, I really don't know, I just don't understand why being the most important country artist of your decade isn't as important or something that you could maintain and then control your acting career.

"But he seems to wanna act no matter what, you know, there—he gets some enjoyment out of it, and acting is difficult, I've asked him that, I said, 'Man, how do you do this?' 'Cause he's not one that's prone to get up at seven in the morning and go sit in makeup and be on the set for fourteen hours, so, there must be something about it that I don't understand."

In short, if you could be Hank Williams. Or Lefty Frizzell. Or Buck Owens. Why would you decide to become Steve Buscemi?

16

The Same Fool

HOWEVER SIGNIFICANT the shift in Yoakam's career focus as he flirted with cinema, there's no question that his position in the world of commercial country music had changed precipitously. He had been a breakout star from the start of his recording career, riding high through "Streets of Bakersfield" and "I Sang Dixie" and soaring even higher with "A Thousand Miles from Nowhere" and "Ain't That Lonely Yet."

And, then, with *Gone*, he was gone—at least from the ranks of the reliable hitmakers, the ones that radio would add right out of the box and keep in power rotation through the climb to the top of the charts. Again, not that anyone connected with the making of *Gone* expresses the slightest reservation about it. It's a daring album, and it's a great one. It's the record Dwight had to make, and it's one that his Nashville label had no idea how to sell, no luck in selling, or no interest in selling.

In the music industry, there's a familiar term, "turntable hit," which is used to describe songs that have gotten tons of airplay (through heavy promotion, even payola) but which never came close to moving commensurate copies at retail. Listeners might think of the song as a hit; the cash register knew better.

For Yoakam, *Gone* was what we might call a "newsstand hit," generating the most press of his career—and some of the most favorable—yet never getting the radio boost that might have extended his string as a country hitmaker. Instead, it ended it.

"Jim Ed Norman had always been a real big champion of me as a producer and for Dwight's career," says Anderson of the head of the Nashville division of Dwight's label. "He was like a cool guy who had lived in L.A. and worked on the Eagles stuff back in the day, and he said, 'Let 'em go. Let 'em do their thing.' And we did. We always made the record that we wanted to make in the fashion that we wanted to make it."

But in the latter half of the 1990s, it became plain that the game-changer in country music was Garth, not Dwight. And those who became the reliable hitmakers in Garth's wake— Alan Jackson, Brooks & Dunn, Tim McGraw, Kenny Chesney, et al.—may have made some good records (you can read diminishing returns in the order of that list), but none were likely to rock the boat the way Dwight did. As long as Dwight sold a ton of product, he was worth the trouble, but as soon as he didn't, he wasn't. There was more money to be made in country music in the 1990s than ever before, but the music had reverted to the sort of formula that Dwight had resisted from the start.

Likely Yoakam was no longer the priority he had once been at Warner Bros. Nashville, which helps explain why 1998's *A Long Way Home* wasn't a huge hit album, though it was plain to those who made it and to listeners who heard it—then or later—that it ranks with one of his best. If the producer and artist were still committed to making "Dwight Yoakam music," that music had again become more recognizably country, conforming to the conventions of the genre, celebrating them rather than challenging them in the way that *Gone* had.

Maybe if Dwight had followed *This Time* with something closer to *A Long Way Home*, he'd still be having hits for a major label, still working with Pete Anderson. But if he'd done that, we wouldn't have *Gone*, an album that was as much of a creative triumph as it was a commercial disappointment.

There was another two-and-a-half-year interval between *Gone* and *A Long Way Home*, as there had been between *This Time* and *Gone*. Such an extended period between albums had become standard in rock, but it was an eternity in the country market, so the artist and his label filled the gap with two releases in 1997, within two months of each other: *Under the Covers* (July) and *Come On Christmas* (September). The latter was the obligatory holiday album, which artists issue in order to sell for years to come, and which, in this case, is very good and very Dwight, if little heard.

The former is strange, even by the standards set by *Gone*. It gave the first American release to a couple of cuts from the *La Croix D'Amour* import ("Here Comes the Night," "Things We Said Today"), returned to the inspiration of Johnny "Honky-Tonk Man" Horton with "North to Alaska," resurrected the Roy Orbison/Everly Brothers classic "Claudette," and offered Dwight's take on a couple of contemporary ballads: Jimmy Webb's "Wichita Lineman" and Danny O' Keefe's "Good Time Charlie's Got the Blues." And Dwight enlisted Sheryl Crow to play Cher to his Sonny for "Baby Don't Go," the kind of duet that might have once provided a crossover hit but wasn't released as a single.

Where most of those cuts played things pretty straight, the radical rearrangement of the Kinks song "Tired of Waiting for

You" sounds like a Rat Pack/Vegas miscalculation that wouldn't have a prayer of connecting with either rock fans or country radio. Explains Anderson, "Dwight came to me and said, 'Man, I want to do something like Louis Prima, kinda swinging.'" And when Pete subsequently heard the Kinks song on the radio, he had an idea for how to give it that feel. Which explains how the track came about, but hardly excuses it.

Equally radical but more successful is the recasting of the Clash's "Train in Vain" as a bluegrass breakdown, featuring banjo and harmonies from Dr. Ralph Stanley. Continues Anderson, "Dwight brought in the bluegrass version of the Clash. He was of the Clash generation. I certainly wasn't. He's younger than me. Nothing against the Clash, but I go from Muddy Waters to Buck Owens."

In addition to these recording projects that didn't make major demands on his songwriting services, Yoakam was filling his time making *The Newton Boys* with Austin director Richard Linklater. The film generated mixed reviews and mainly seemed to give the director a chance to work with his buddies Matthew McConaughey and Ethan Hawke, who overshadowed Yoakam.

Roger Ebert wrote in the *Chicago Sun-Times*, "Dwight Yoakam is their explosives expert, who pours nitro as if intensely curious about what it would feel like to be vaporized in the next nanosecond." Janet Maslin's review in the *New York Times* offers, "The film is often straightforward bordering on sedate. (Dwight Yoakam and Chloe Webb, as the group's nitroglycerine expert and his insinuating wife, seem to have wandered in from a kinkier, possibly more interesting movie.)"

Both Linklater and Yoakam would recover. And if the movie didn't do much to raise Yoakam's thespian profile, the down time that making a movie involves made him more prolific than ever as a songwriter. *A Long Way Home* was the first (and rare) Yoakam album to credit all material solely to the artist. And the consistently high level of the writing suggests that, if anything, making movies was having a beneficial effect on Yoakam's music.

Yoakam agrees. "Yeah. Absolutely. I wrote some of the best material I've ever written while shooting in Austin, Texas. Just waiting around a lot, you'd have days when you're just staring out at the Colorado River. [He starts playing the intro to the album opening "Same Fool"]. So, I think I wrote more. Because touring interrupts writing. Writing is stationary; it allows me to ponder and think outside myself. And I'd hope I was getting better at it. *A Long Way Home* had thirteen songs on it, and they were all mine. First one where I had no covers."

If we reconsider Dwight's journey a metaphor for his music, the full-circle implications of this title are plain, suggesting how far he'd strayed from the straight and narrow on previous releases. "And with *A Long Way Home*, we knew we'd probably taken it as far as it could go," he agrees. "I'm proud of the other things, but . . . you could feel that the journey was completed."

While in no way a repudiation of the detours, side trips, and creative skyrocketing that had come before, *A Long Way Home* suggests a return to traditional country classicism, reinforcing that Dwight was the same guy (or the "Same Fool," as he sings in his most Buck Owens–esque phrasing) who made *Guitars, Cadillacs* and *Hillbilly Deluxe*. It could have passed as a natural progression from those.

It's also far lighter (not lightweight, but buoyant) than the noirish streak that ran from *Buenas Noches* through *This Time* and *Gone*. Even the design of the packaging is whiter and brighter, recalling the early days, while the (airbrushed?) photos of Dwight appear to have turned back the hands of time. In his early forties when making the album, Yoakam could have passed in these photos for mid-twenties.

Though the road of love remains rocky in Yoakam's material, the arrangements reinforce the lighter touch. The lyric to the title track is one of Yoakam's best in haiku mystic mode ("Hate is deep, and its pull is strong. But the passion's short, then it's a long way home."), but the melody suggests something out of the Lovin' Spoonful. And the Chet Atkins–style picking of "These Arms" recalls that goodtime band's "Nashville Cats," which of course was homage to an era of country classicism.

The opening steel run of "Same Fool" evokes the "Rainy Day Woman" of Waylon Jennings, the following "The Curse" proceeds at a Johnny Cash lope, and the majestic "Things Change" and the string-laden "Yet to Succeed" rank with definitive Dwight. Everything he'd ever done well before, he did as well or better here—even out-punking the adrenalin fury of "Please, Please Baby" with "Only Want You More," which is reprised as the final "Maybe You Like It, Maybe You Don't" as an unmistakable Elvis Presley impersonation.

"A Long Way Home was one of my favorites, the last full album I worked on with them," says Dusty Wakeman. "There's a real introspective, retrospective quality to that album. As soon as I heard the title cut, I knew what that album was about. And Dwight was really involved in the production of that record. It was a great last record for me to be involved with, because it kind of summed up those nine records."

Listen to his albums out of sequence, and you'd be hard pressed to determine exactly where A Long Way Home fits chronologically or how well it fared commercially. If it had come a decade earlier, "Things Change" and the Buck Owens–style roadhouse shuffle, "These Arms," might have ranked with the biggest hits of Yoakam's career. Instead, the former barely crept into the country top twenty while the latter hardly registered a blip with country radio.

Where Dwight says that, with this album "the journey was completed," it's also plain in retrospect that the game was over. And, as he acknowledged in the hit that should have been, "Things Change"—record companies, producers, management, airplay (or lack thereof), tours. Maybe Dwight himself didn't change much, except for the inevitability of aging amid a country market skewing increasingly younger, but everything around him did. And would, even more, in the years to come.

17

Playing Out the String

ONCE DWIGHT YOAKAM was no longer a hit-generating recording artist for Nashville's Warner Bros./Reprise, it was inevitable that he would no longer be a recording artist with that major label. A rock act or an indie act can sustain a recording career through touring and a loyal fan base, but the country music industry in particular needs hits to feed the beast. And it needs radio to generate hits. No radio, no hits, no major-label recording contract.

Perhaps just as inevitably, once the partnership between Yoakam and his label dissolved, so would the one between the artist and his producer. And in both cases, it's a question of whether there is blame to place or this is just the natural arc of a career. Dwight, Pete, and Warner Bros. had a good run together—a history-making run. But all good things must come to an end.

"Maybe we went about four albums too long," says Dwight of his collaboration with Anderson. "But that happens, and I'm proud of everything we did together. Things just ran their course."

And without allowing this book to degenerate into the sort of "he said/he said" dispute that Yoakam and his management might have feared, we have to at least acknowledge a different perspective on the part of the producer: "I personally don't think so," says Anderson of any suggestion that he was no longer the right producer for Dwight. "But I can only grow as much as the artist grows . . . Maybe Dwight stopped bringing his 'A' game. And maybe I'm not the easiest guy to be around. But what producer is gonna come in and make Dwight better than *Gone* or *This Time*? Guess what? It ain't gonna happen! T Bone Burnett, Don Was, any of my contemporaries? Ain't gonna happen. What are they gonna know about Dwight and bring to the table that I didn't?"

Dusty Wakeman remains friends with both, and can see both sides, yet finds it hard to agree with Dwight if that four albums of counting backwards includes the last one Wakeman worked on.

"You know, careers have an arc," he says. "That's the way it works. They later made some albums I wasn't involved in and perhaps they'd worn each other out by then. But I thought *A Long Way Home* was as good a record as *Gone* was. They may not have been as warm and fuzzy as they once were, but I think the team was still working well together."

Whatever the verdict, the hits had come to an end before the contract would, which meant there were still four more releases by Dwight on Warner Bros./Reprise, and Pete would produce all of them. But only one could be considered a real album of new material—2000's millennially titled *Tomorrow's Sounds Today*. And, to my ears, this was the first (and last) album by Dwight that would simply sound like product, as if he had gone to this particular well a little too often.

Preceding that was a(nother) greatest hits album, with too few hits. Following *Tomorrow's Sounds Today* was an unplugged (and generally if unfairly ignored) solo album, *dwightyoakam acoustic.net*. Capping his Warner Bros. decades was a soundtrack that nobody heard to a film nobody saw. And then, again inevitably, there was the four-disc box set, the tombstone to Dwight's days (till then) as a major-label recording artist, documenting just how high he had skyrocketed and how fast he had fallen. It also demonstrated how tough it was to encapsulate his musical progression as a collection of hits, highlights, and outtakes, because Dwight's best albums demand and deserve to be heard as albums.

But since Dwight had pretty much written himself out with *A Long Way Home*, and was finding his focus on film sharpening as his country career was faltering, there would be another gap of more than two years before *Tomorrow's Sounds Today*. And since country music, like nature, abhors a vacuum, that gap would need to be filled, and was, with the May 1999 release of the expansively titled *Last Chance for a Thousand Years: Dwight Yoakam's Greatest Hits from the '90s*.

The generous selection of fourteen cuts was designed to appeal to two very different groups. First, those who were a little curious about Dwight and had heard him on the radio, but hadn't been among the three million–plus that popped for *This Time*, the album where four of these hits had previously appeared. At the other extreme were the Dwight fanatics, the completists, the true believers, the ones who would need the compilation for the three previously unreleased tracks, even though they already owned the rest.

In comparison with Yoakam's previous hits collection released ten years earlier, *Last Chance* boasted some of his biggest hits, ones that had extended his musical reach well beyond the confines of country. Yet there weren't as many of them, and all of the eight that could remotely qualify as country radio hits were from just two albums (with four from *If There Was a Way* as well).

Curiously, the three new tracks from very different sources all supplied what Yoakam's own material lacked: a positive perspective on love. "Thinking About Leaving" would never be a single, let alone a hit, but the ballad possessed an impressive pedigree, as the only released co-write between Yoakam and Rodney Crowell, the renowned singer-songwriter who had also enjoyed a string of chart-topping country hits pre-Garth. You can hear the distinctive styles of both of them in the song (which, despite its title, is more about staying), with Crowell in particular on the bridge.

The second of the unreleased studio tracks is "I'll Go Back to Her," a Waylon Jennings obscurity that barely registered any impact through Yoakam's rendition. Yet the third and most surprising selection would spur sales of the compilation and give Yoakam new commercial life as both a country and crossover artist. "Yoakam sings Queen" wouldn't seem like a surefire gambit for a career resurgence, but the rockabilly spirit of "Crazy Little Thing Called Love" suited Yoakam even better than it had Freddie Mercury.

So the good news was that Dwight was back on the radio, back on the charts, back in the public eye as a recording artist (and pitchman, with the song commissioned for a Gap commercial). The bad news, for a visionary artist who considered songwriting one of his main strengths, was that the public responded more strongly to taking a Queen tune for a retro spin than it had to any of his original material for a long five years.

Few artists paid closer attention to image than Yoakam, who generally took or shared credit for art direction on his albums, so the western motif of the hits package reflected a significant shift and offered a hint of the film project that would soon consume him. Stetson aside, Yoakam had never been known as much of a cowboy (since ranches were in short supply in both the Hollywood Hills where he lived and rust-belt Ohio where he was raised), but the CD booklet showed a soft focus Dwight on horseback, gazing wistfully into the distance. The black-and-white CD cover features a close-up of galloping hooves.

Wherever Dwight's career was galloping, the release of *Tomorrow's Sounds Today* in October 2000 found Dwight and Pete limping toward the finish line of Yoakam's recording contract with Warner Bros. Nashville. Though a film soundtrack would follow, this would be the last album on a major label by Dwight Yoakam to be targeted at country radio. And radio would turn a deaf ear, with only the Buddy Hollyesque "What Do You Know About Love" making a minor ripple (without cracking the top twenty).

It isn't a bad album by the standards of that era's country music, but it was a decidedly desultory affair by Dwight's and Pete's. Where his creative peak of the mid-1990s had found Yoakam in expansive mode, pushing limits and transcending boundaries, *Tomorrow's Sounds Today*, like the superior *A Long Way Home* before it, is an album of retrenchment, one that reinforces Yoakam's persona as a country artist rather than extending it, with too many of the cuts sounding like retreads.

"At this stage, Dwight definitely had his identity set in stone and he had his two or three or four directions he could go in as a singer/artist/writer," says Anderson. "Then it was up to me not to repeat the same tricks again as an arranger."

The major trick on this album is the elevation of pedal steel guitarist Gary Morse into a spotlight position as a foil for Anderson's electric guitar. It was like a third element, turning the call-and-response relationship between Yoakam's voice and Anderson's guitar, long the focus of the musical dynamic, into something closer to tripart. Anderson and Morse, who had begun recording with Yoakam during the sessions for the new tracks on the last hits package, found a fresh interplay as they framed the vocal.

More steel meant more country, as attested by titles such as "A Place to Cry" and "The Heartaches Are Free" (the latter the closest that Yoakam would ever come to channeling Hank Williams, though he sounded more like an actor in a role). Yet the steel would also play a prominent role in the album's major curve ball, a version of Cheap Trick's "I Want You to Want Me" that is as inspired as it is unlikely, making the band's own break-out hit seem lightweight by comparison. Here and elsewhere on the album, Yoakam showed that he still had what it took to connect with a song and a mainstream audience. Yet, again, there had to be some concern that the material bringing out the best in him came from the likes of Queen and Cheap Trick.

Reinforcing the album's thrown-together, tossed-off feel are the two concluding "Bonus Bucks," reuniting the artist with mentor Owens. Since the musical quality couldn't qualify as highlights, and didn't really fit with the rest, they were simply tacked onto the end. "Alright, I'm Wrong" got Anderson his first writing credit on a Yoakam album, with an accordion-driven cantina number that sounds like the Texas Tornados (with Buck's vocal sounding like it was phoned in), though the closing revival of Buck's "I Was There" makes more of an impact.

The album didn't, except for the Cheap Trick cover as a cu-riosity among rock fans. If Yoakam and Warner Bros. hadn't previously given up on each other, they plainly did in the after-math of his last full-fledged, full-band studio album. Big deal. Dwight had a movie to do, one into which he had been pouring all of his creative energies, placing his entire bankroll on a long shot. Boom or bust.

18

South of Heaven, West of Hell (and Off the Charts)

PLEASE FORGIVE THE chronological hiccup. Preceding *Tomorrow's Sounds Today* was the stealth release of the solo *dwightyoa kamacoustic.net* just five months earlier, but it made more thematic sense for us to jump from the *Last Chance for a Thousand Years* hits package directly into *Tomorrow's Sounds* and save the unplugged album for this chapter with the soundtrack on Dwight's end of the line with Warner Bros. Because unless you're a Dwight diehard, these are the two albums you never even knew existed.

The hits package and *Tomorrow's Sounds Today* were both reflective of Dwight's association with a major label, and both were intended to generate power-rotation airplay and to achieve massive mainstream sales. That neither did turned the strains in Yoakam's relationship with his label into a rupture beyond healing, but at least those releases gave the impression, or sustained the illusion, of business as usual.

By contrast, *dwightyoakamacoustic.net* and the *South of Heaven, West of Hell* soundtrack were more like boutique projects or vanity recordings, released without any marketing muscle whatsoever, little known among country fans who might have still considered themselves among Yoakam's core constituency. Thus, they went barely heard, though among the few who heard them, they rank with Dwight's most inspired efforts.

An attempt to both jump on the "unplugged" bandwagon and to connect with the early (by country standards) Internet adopters, the solo album stands as a crucial cornerstone in an appreciation of Yoakam's talent, as indispensable as the early Roxy live set belatedly released with the deluxe edition of *Guitars, Cadillacs*.

Because in an era that had become dominated by pretty young faces, lyrical clichés, and assembly-line production, Yoakam still had to face accusations that he was something other than the real deal, that he was a phony playing the role of a country purist (while twitching his butt to elicit female squeals).

With a full complement of twenty-five numbers of solo acoustic performance (producer Anderson provides electric guitar accompaniment only on a reshuffled "Little Sister"), the album is a tour de force of vocal virtuosity, a revelation in terms of the power of Yoakam's rhythm guitar, and a testament to a talent that not only drew from the icons of country's classic past, but could hold its own with them.

As Anderson would later insist, years after a lawsuit would end any relationship or even conversation between the two of them, "I don't care, you take anybody. Take Lefty, take Hank, take Merle. And you set them in a room and put Yoakam in there, and give him an acoustic guitar. And you're gonna go, 'Whoa, this guy's right up there!'"

Though Pete produced it, the album serves as a response to those who might think that Yoakam's success was primarily a result of Anderson's production. Strip everything away and you've got those songs, that voice, the qualities that convinced crucial supporters at an early stage that Yoakam had what it took to be a big country star. And though the solo acoustic arrangements here ensured that country radio would never touch this, it provides evidence of the enduring power of those songs and that voice, all the way to the a cappella finale of "Guitars, Cadillacs."

Along the way, it inspires some reassessment. In the solo acoustic rendition, "Readin', Rightin', Rt. 23" sounds monumental and deeply heartfelt, with not a hint of anachronism. On the other hand, "A Thousand Miles from Nowhere," a smash that would expand Yoakam's musical world significantly, offers barely an indication of the majesty it achieved through its studio arrangement. Nice tune, but you wouldn't necessarily single it out as a highlight amid the strong, more traditional competition surrounding it.

With a full-fledged studio album in the pipeline, set for release just months ahead, the label (and the artist) didn't want the marketplace confused, so there was little attempt to make anyone aware of the release. Yet it remained a nice souvenir for diehard fans and is a revelation for those who subsequently happen upon it.

And its credits provided cross promotion for his website (www.dwightyoakam.net), as well as the one for his burgeoning biscuit company (www.bakersfieldbiscuits.com, where you can still find an array of selections ranging from chicken fries to breakfast burritos in "Dwight Yoakam's Family of Quality Foods").

With *Sling Blade*, *The Newton Boys*, and a couple of lesser TV roles under his belt, Yoakam had plainly been bitten by the acting bug, and perhaps was considering this a more viable medium in which to age gracefully and mature creatively, particularly now that his recording career had plummeted from its chart-topping peak. If he had sounded a little distracted on the offhand *Tomorrow's Sounds Today*, he was plainly preoccupied with *South of Heaven, West of Hell*—a film written, directed, and produced by Dwight Yoakam, starring Dwight Yoakam, with music by Dwight Yoakam.

Maybe Yoakam hoped the movie would do for him what *Sling Blade* had done for his buddy Billy Bob Thornton, who had also leapt from the bandstand to the big screen, was attempting to balance the two careers, and was riding shotgun on Dwight's film. Other noteworthies among the cast included Peter and Bridget Fonda, Paul "Pee-wee Herman" Reubens, a moonlighting Warren Zevon (payback for "Carmelita"?), and an emerging Vince Vaughn.

"He asked me to be in his movie, which was unfortunately an ill-fated experience for him," says Texas roadhouse mainstay Joe Ely. "He would have so many takes of the same scene that everybody wondered how he was going to make it through. But he was such a perfectionist, he wanted it to be exactly the way he saw it. And by doing that, I think that's what made him run out of money and lose control of the project. Somebody else took it over because he couldn't finish the movie. I wish that he could have, because it was an interesting twist on a Western, but whoever took it over edited the real story completely out of it."

Wherever credit or blame is due, the finished product wasn't widely released or reviewed, and the few aware of it critiqued it as incomprehensible or called it a vanity project. There are even conflicting dates for the release, 2000 or 2001, since it mainly bypassed the big screen and went straight to the small, for home consumption. *TV Guide* dismissed it as "what happens when grown-ups with more money than inspiration get the notion to dress up like cowboys and bandits and make their own variation on *The Wild Bunch* (1969), with vaguely supernatural undertones."

And despite Pete Anderson's earlier advice that Dwight make a singing cowboy movie that might pay promotional dividends for their music careers, this wasn't exactly what he had in mind: "We had discussions about it, and I encouraged him about his scriptwriting and his writing abilities," says Anderson. "He'd started a film company with Billy Bob Thornton, and I thought it was a great opportunity for the two of them. But I said, 'Just don't be in it.' That'll come later. Have a little film company and develop something and get your name away from the splatter if it blows up. If you write, direct, produce, act, tap dance, costume—man, every finger's going to point at you if it's not successful. And there's so many reasons why something cannot be successful other than its quality. Which we had learned in the music business."

A soundtrack to a hit movie might generate a hit single or two, but the 2001 album "with songs and score from and inspired by the motion picture" met the same fate as the film. It never even cracked the country music Top 50 on *Billboard* charts. It marked the end of the Warner Bros. contract. Yet some of the few who have heard it place it with Yoakam's best music.

"Minus the nine snippets of film dialogue interspersed throughout, it ranks as one of the artist's deepest, most stirring albums," opines David McGee in *The New Rolling Stone Record Guide* (2004), and goes on to praise one of the tracks, "Somewhere," as "an instant Yoakam classic."

Like the tree falling unheard in the woods, can a song be a classic if known to no one? Yet the music merits wider exposure, despite how inscrutable those inserted bits of dialogue will sound to those who haven't seen the film—in other words, almost everyone. In addition to bringing the West back into country and western, the music steeps itself in both gospel and Southern rock. Rarely had Dwight illuminated the religious underpinnings of his music as brightly as he did on "Who at the Door Is Standing" and "The Darkest Hour." Rarely had he rocked as hard as he did on "The First Thing Smokin'" or evoked the era of the Allman Brothers as strongly as on "No Future in Sight."

Both served to showcase the guitar of Anderson, the album's producer. In retrospect, it might have made sense—or at least been a neater split—for the artist and producer to end their relationship with the end of the major-label contract. Unless Dwight signed with another major, he would be less likely to have any shot at radio and require the services of a producer well compensated for the previous commercial success they'd enjoyed together. And if Dwight was as interested or more interested in making movies, there was less opportunity to hit the road, where playing guitar on tour remained Anderson's major passion.

"With the Warner career over, maybe it would have been a good time to leave. But it would be like, 'Once you don't have Warner Bros. on your side, Pete's gonna quit'?" hypothetically asks Anderson, who doesn't consider himself a quitter.

So when Dwight signed to Audium/Koch, which treated him as a huge priority (after he'd become an afterthought for Warner), but lacked the muscle to get him the radio play that would re-establish him, Pete continued as Yoakam's producer, with a budget considerably downsized from Dwight's latter albums with Warner (where the budget had already been downsized in light of the artist's commercial descent).

"After losing his deal with Warner Bros., he thought he had a shot that was more than what it was with Audium/Koch," continues Anderson. "I thought we could make a great record, but I didn't think they could get us on the radio. 'Cause that's a political thing. Dwight could have songs on the radio every day, and people would love them. It's not a question of quality. It's arm twisting and money and all that other bullshit."

Maybe Anderson should have seen the album's title, *Population: Me*, as prophecy. Not that *Population: Me and Pete* would have been as catchy, but it was hard to resist the implication of the lone man making a last stand against the world. Not the two as a team, the way it had begun, when each was bolstering the other's confidence while the rest of the world didn't pay much attention or share any faith.

As the only album of new material Dwight would record for the indie label, the 2003 release calls in some significant markers in terms of guest support, with Willie Nelson contributing a duet vocal on "If Teardrops Were Diamonds," Timothy B. Schmit of the Eagles providing harmonies throughout, and the venerable banjo virtuoso Earl Scruggs helping Yoakam transform the Burt Bacharach standard "Trains and Boats and Planes." Even if the budget was indie, the credits aimed at a higher profile.

The results were promising, more inspired than the lackluster *Tomorrow's Sounds Today*. In a departure from precedent, Yoakam aligned himself with the alt-country flank that looked up to him the way that he'd always looked up to Buck Owens and Johnny Horton, opening the album with the stirring anthem "The Late Great Golden State" by the young Los Angeles singer-songwriter Mike Stinson. Those who don't read credits would have mistaken it for one of Yoakam's own, even one of his best.

"I ain't old, I'm just out of date," sings Yoakam with a mixture of defiance and regret, amid an arrangement with the buoyancy of up-tempo Eagles, while the lyric laments that the era of country-rocking at the Palomino is long gone.

Writer Stinson remembers Yoakam coming to one of his club dates because the girlfriends of the two were close. Dwight plainly heard echoes of his earlier days in the lesser-known artist's musical dynamic.

"Incidentally it was the same night that Dwight met Keith Gattis, who went on to play guitar in Dwight's band for a few years," says Stinson. "Well, Dwight loved the show and was super cool and encouraging to me and the band. He gave me his number and said, 'Let me know when you're playing.'

"Man, I left that gig walking one foot off the ground! I mean, this was the guy who saved '80's country music all by himself, the coolest cowboy singer to come along in a couple of decades. I had every record he'd made and had seen him live several times, the first bona fide musical hero of mine to attend one of my shows. And in my opinion, no finer songwriter could have walked through that door and liked my show either."

Things got better for Stinson when he heard that Dwight had bought a copy of his album at Amoeba Records in Hollywood. And better still when Dwight said he wanted to record the cut, make it the kickoff track on the album, and even ended up playing it on *The Tonight Show*. It was like another passing of the torch, with Dwight now the established veteran giving a boost to the up-and-comer.

"How often does your work get validated by one of the true masters of your craft?" continues Stinson. "I could have died and gone to Houston right then! That song has paid a lot of rent and a lot of bills for a lot of years. And he gave my credibility a bump that it sorely needed."

Like "Late Great Golden State," the album's title cut continues that theme of last man standing, in a song so forlorn it could have fit amid the darkness of *Gone*, and with an arrangement that mixes banjo (more prevalent on this album than ever before) with what sounds like tuba (though there are no credits for such). The sound of the album and its songs seem like something of a fresh start for Yoakam, unbroken after his demotion from the major-label ranks.

"I'm proud of that last record we made," says Anderson. "It was made under more constraints, because we didn't have the budget we'd had. It was close to a third, much less than half, of what we'd had from Warner. And I was there every day, overseeing every penny, every note. If you thought we were working hard before, now we really have to work hard.

"I come from blue-collar working class and I want to get it done," he continues. "I don't want to be lighting candles and caring about who's doing the catering. We've been given a great opportunity, let's get in here and do the job. And Dwight's the same way. He always focused and worked hard in the studio."

So the studio sessions gave no indication that this would be their last project together, at least not in Anderson's mind. The budget was tighter, but otherwise it was business as usual. The rupture would come in the album's wake, when Dwight resumed touring, following an extended hiatus from the road while focusing on *South of Heaven, West of Hell*. This time, he'd decided to go out without Pete and the band.

19

Splitsville

AFTER TWO DECADES, the relationship ended not with a bang or a whimper, but with a flurry of faxes. Pete's were scrawled in furious Sharpie. Such was his response to the news that Dwight had decided to tour again in support of *Population: Me*, but that he'd be going out with a stripped-down two-piece instead of Anderson and band.

Maybe there were musical reasons for the decision, but certainly there were financial ones. Yoakam had made a substantial investment—financially and professionally—in *South of Heaven, West of Hell*. And he hadn't recouped. To the contrary, the movie had reportedly been taken away from him when he could no longer pay the bills.

It's a whole lot cheaper to hit the road with a couple of musicians than it is to mount a full tour with a full band. And if fans were paying to see Dwight Yoakam, maybe they wouldn't care and maybe as many of them would show up anyway. But for a guy like Pete, the decision not only left a big hole in his calendar and his bank account, it deprived him of what he loved to do most—go out and play the guitar.

"Dwight had told me he wasn't going to tour," says Anderson. "I'd lost a month of work the previous year [because of the film], but it was always like, 'This is a long-term relationship and we'll catch up, something's gonna happen.' And then he wanted to go out with a duo because he needed to make some money.

"So he toured for the summer [of 2003] after saying he wasn't going to tour, and I sent him a fax that said I'm out X amount of dollars, a big pile of money. And they made a counteroffer that was really weak. It escalated from there, and then we settled out of court. And now all's good. I can separate business from friendship and relationships. There was the music, there was the making of the records, but there was also the touring behind the records. Those were two separate things, and I had a deal to tour."

It's worth noting again that Dwight has nothing bad to say about Pete for publication, and that Pete really doesn't have anything bad to say about Dwight, except his disappointment over the way things ended. Maybe they didn't need to end. Maybe, as Dwight has suggested, they should have ended earlier. Though neither Dwight nor Pete has enjoyed anything near the commercial success apart that they shared at their peak, both the art and the commerce were on the decline during their last years with Warner Bros., well before the split. Maybe it's just the arc of a career—you rise, you fall. You get older. You develop different interests and goals. You grow in different directions.

"I wish it had been a more amicable split," says Dwight. "But you know what? I'm proud of everything we did together. And I'll always feel that my music is better for having known him. Would I have been more or less without Pete? I don't know, because it didn't happen any other way.

"It would have been different, that's all. In some ways. In some ways not. You hear the demo, you hear the record. What he was able to do was pull a tight focus on technical aspects, what we were going to do in terms of execution. And that allowed me great freedom as a song creator and singer. And he allowed you your say—it was a collaborative effort. But things ran their course, and it was time for us to work outside of one another."

Maybe more than money was involved, as even Pete acknowledges.

"If I had to make my guess, he probably got tired of me being Pete," says Anderson. "Or his feeling constrained that he couldn't produce himself."

Anderson insists that money shouldn't have been the stumbling block, that he was prepared to make short-term sacrifices for the sake of the long-term relationship. And that he would have convinced the band to do the same.

"When he said he needed to make a little money to pay off the film and blah blah blah, I said, 'I know I'm making a lot of money,'" remembers Anderson. "'Would you like me to adjust my earnings, call the guys, go down to a four piece?' Basically, 'Do you want me to help you to get out of this?'

"I had a position of obligation in my mind," he continues. "I could have gotten the band to say, 'Let's have everybody go out on tour for expenses and get Dwight out of debt. And when it's over, you'll be paid back in spades.' But that just isn't what he wanted to do. In his mind, what he wanted to do is exactly what he did. He wanted to go do his own thing the way he did it. He didn't want me around anymore. There could have been a better way to say it, but okay. It's not like I dwell on it or lose sleep over it."

The split offers another chance to assess what each of them brought to the table, though the differences in Yoakam's music aren't as significant after Pete, when the artist began producing himself, as they were before Pete.

By all accounts, including their own, the two were both strong willed and like-minded, and they shared a vision of how the music should sound and how it should progress, rarely butting heads in the studio. Even to the end, Anderson remembers few cross words. Any frustrations were generally put aside for the sake of the bigger picture.

"There was never tension, up to the very end, that I noticed," insists Anderson. "The working relationship was always the same. In twenty years of working together, we only had cross times once or twice in the studio, where I got really frustrated or something. We were aware of, like, Keith and Mick and, like, Buck and Don. And after Don [Rich, a guitarist and harmonizer with Buck Owens] passed, what happened to Buck. So Dwight was cognizant of that. This works."

Until, in Dwight's mind, it didn't. Maybe some of that's a result of growing up. After a couple of decades together, the nine-year age gap and the original contrast in experience didn't seem to mean as much. Pete could hardly remain the mentor he had been in the beginning. But likely a bigger part was diminishing returns, the lack of hits and radio play, a commercial decline that was all but inevitable for a country artist of Yoakam's generation. Hell, even Vince Gill, the ultimate company man, nice guy, and hit machine (and an extremely gifted guitarist and vocalist), was feeling those same frustrations with a fall from commercial grace.

"I knew the music was great," says Anderson. "But there was starting to really not be a radio format for us anyway." Too old for contemporary country, too young for oldies (not that the classic country format has much traction anyway).

It's fitting that the relationship would rupture over touring rather than recording. Neither Dwight nor Pete (nor those who worked with them) recalled serious disagreements in the studio. The division of labor remained clear: Dwight wrote and sang the songs; Pete arranged and produced the music. As long as those lines weren't crossed, there was no need to argue, and as long as the records kept selling more and more each time, there was no need to cross those lines.

Yet Pete insists that his first love all along was playing the guitar, preferably in front of an audience. And that even though his work with Dwight established him foremost as a producer, his aim from the time he started working with Dwight was to ensure himself plenty of opportunity to pursue that first love.

"To be truthfully honest, everything I ever did was to play guitar," he says. "That's all I ever wanted to do. Producing came easy for me. Guitar playing was difficult; I practiced really hard. Because I loved it. I'd been in bands way before Dwight, but you can't speak up when there's five supposed equals in a room. You're just the guitar player, you can't tell the drummer what to do. And once I got the clipboard that had my notes on it, I called that the mantle of authority. Once Dwight gave me the mantle of authority—'Pete's producing this'—I had no problem telling people what to do or what to play."

Pete's success with Dwight led to other offers to provide similar direction for other artists, leading to a career he'd had no intention to pursue: "After Dwight's first record, Warner Bros. asked if I'd do a record with Rosie Flores," he continues. "And I knew Rosie, we were pals, but I really didn't want to do it. Even after Dwight's record was successful, I think I was still sorting out what a producer was, to be honest with you. I hadn't figured out how this was a job and you made money.

"So once I made the record with Dwight, it was like, let's go out and tour the world. I want everybody to hear me play guitar. And then they came to me and said, 'We'll give you $25,000 to produce Rosie,' which at that time could have been a million dollars. So I said, 'Sure, I'll take it.' Then I started to formulate what a producer was. But, yeah, Dwight's success meant everything for my world as a producer. It was a rocket launch."

The rocket launch subsequently led *Rolling Stone* to dub Anderson its "hot producer" in an annual "Hot" issue, for his work with Michelle Shocked as well as the Dwight hits, and he eventually amassed production credits that extended from Steve Forbert to the Meat Puppets. He also became a mini-mogul, signing artists and producing them for his Little Dog Records. Yet he never felt he spread himself so thin that his work with Dwight suffered. (And when his studio commitments kept him from the road, the late Eddy Shaver provided an electrifying replacement, and many Dwight fans might not have even known the difference.)

"I kinda wanted to have my cake and eat it too," admits Pete. "Producing records was cool, but I really didn't look on it as much of a job. And then eventually it became a job. And it's odd that I probably made a name more for myself as a producer than a guitarist. But Dwight's records were always the high-water mark, because I was so involved with them.

"The good thing for Dwight's career was that everything I learned on someone else's sessions I would bring to his next record. I started to understand all the things that would make the records better, production-wise, and more competitive. I learned how competitive sonics were in record making. And we made our records definitely from a rock, West Coast perspective, not from a Nashville perspective. We made them like we were rock and roll guys."

How involved was Dwight in the sound of Dwight Yoakam's music? The artist and the producer started out with a single vision, using Buck Owens and Don Rich as the model. Success encouraged them to extend their aural horizons, and such progression brought more success. Pete always knew that they were Dwight's songs, his voice, his album, his baby—and that one of the producer's main mandates is to please the artist. And the busier that Dwight got with acting, the more responsibility Pete assumed for thinking for both of them.

"As much as Dwight was paying attention, he trusted Pete to do what Pete was going to do," recalls Dusty Wakeman. "It wasn't like Dwight was sitting there all the time. He was pretty much not there except for vocal time or when we had a guest star come in to play. With the building and framing the house, he just trusted us. And he'd come in when the decorator was there, you know what I mean?

"And Dwight's a guy who on any given day can come in and do an amazing vocal on a couple of passes," continues Wakeman. "By the second batch of records, he'd gotten into the acting thing, plus these guys were touring like crazy. So he had a lot on his plate besides just making the records. The big picture focus was there, but day to day—when he'd been on the phone with managers and agents all morning—it was hard for him to shut that down and say, 'Okay, I'm gonna sing now.'

"It would take more time to get his vocals done, because he might have been talking for three hours, and his voice was tired. And with his voice, it's like there's 90 percent and there's 100 percent. And everybody else might be perfectly happy with his 90 percent, but he wouldn't be."

So, the pair of ambitious, hard-working perfectionists made a perfect team, as long as the records were selling and radio was playing them and Dwight was receiving positive response for his film endeavors. When the major-label recording career tanked and Dwight lost his shirt on his film, it was time to question a relationship that had been impervious to challenge from the start. Even Pete knew that things had to change. He just figured he'd still be an integral part of that change. And he proposed a big idea about how to keep the show rolling while circumventing the normal channels of record labels and radio play.

"I had this idea for this thing with the working title *The Death of Country Music*," says Pete. "I wanted to do a stage play. What you needed was something he didn't have to write any new material for but would be great in and attract a lot of attention. Something a little different from the usual record-tour routine. So, you have this stage play, and you start it with Jimmie Rodgers, the Singing Brakeman, and you end it with Merle Haggard. And go through five guys, loosely, from Jimmie to Hank to Lefty to Buck to Merle, something like that. Because after Merle, it was over.

"So you'd have a stage play, a DVD, a soundtrack record, then wrap that up and go play casinos. We'd do a set of each guy and end with Dwight Yoakam music. And that could be a two or three year turnaround, and you could go back to it whenever you wanted to. And he could act in it, being Hank in the back of a Cadillac. But he wasn't interested."

Despite Pete's attempt to suggest a vehicle in which Dwight could combine music and acting, such a project would seem to be a creative dead end. And if Dwight didn't have any more country hits in him—due to changing demographics, record company politics, promotional budgets, and a variety of different factors that have little to do with the quality of music—he felt that he still had plenty of songs to write. And a loyal audience that would continue to support him. And a musical future without Pete Anderson. (Though increasingly it has been in casinos, which pay well for established country names.)

Pete sued, Dwight settled, and that was that. They don't talk, though others who knew them together remain friends with both. Neither sees much possibility of ever working together again.

And the music they made together?

"It's timeless," says Dusty Wakeman, who had the closest view of the collaboration at its peak. "Those guys made history."

20

Produced by Dwight Yoakam

IF *POPULATION: ME* REPRESENTED something of a fresh start for Dwight, *Blame the Vain* was an even fresher one. After a couple of decades of continuity with a major, he'd jumped from one indie deal to another, this time with New West, an artist-friendly label with offices in both Los Angeles and Austin. The latter city had long positioned itself as the anti-Nashville, the place where rougher-hewn creativity resisted the assembly-line polishing of the mainstream country machine.

New West would establish itself as the premier indie label for the emerging "Americana" movement after the turn of the millennium, cornering the market on this artistry much as Rounder had with folk in earlier decades. It provided refuge for artists who had once enjoyed Nashville country success (Kris Kristofferson, Steve Earle), for artists who resisted categorical niches (John Hiatt, Delbert McClinton, the reunion of the Flatlanders with Joe Ely, Butch Hancock, and Jimmie Dale

Gilmore), and for artists who came to twang with a younger perspective (Drive-By Truckers, the Old 97's).

The label also launched a series in association with the *Austin City Limits* program, releasing classic performances (including an early one of Yoakam's) on CD and DVD. And it would subsequently enjoy great success with the Oscar-winning music from the *Crazy Heart* soundtrack, a film steeped in the honky-tonks.

Label head Cameron Strang didn't need to think twice when the opportunity to work with Yoakam presented itself. "For me, this was a total no-brainer," he says. "I'm just a huge fan. When I was running the label there were a few artists who I felt that if I could just sign that person, how fantastic would that be."

Yoakam could have been the biggest commercial catch for the label, but it was never a natural fit. Yes, New West could offer him complete creative freedom, but so had Warner Bros. New West had no connection to country radio and the country music industry at large, and that's still where Dwight's commercial significance lay. What had made him singular was his ability to straddle mainstream country and progressive Americana.

Now he fell into the gulf in between, no longer a major-label hitmaker, but also lacking the stature in Americana circles accorded not only some of his New West label mates—Buddy Miller, in particular—but also creatively rejuvenated artists such as Rodney Crowell, Rosanne Cash, Emmylou Harris, and others who had given up on making music for country radio and were making some of the most inspired music of their careers—for themselves. Even the venerable Johnny Cash had been taking radical chances with his music, recording with cutting-edge producer Rick Rubin, covering material from the likes of Nine Inch Nails.

By contrast, Yoakam still had his ear toward country radio—a commercial ambition that made Americana suspicious. But trying to invade that mainstream music monolith from an indie outpost was like attacking a fortress with a slingshot. New West had no connection to country radio, and fans of Americana were but a fraction of Yoakam's former constituency.

He certainly hadn't broadened that constituency with the 2004 release of *Dwight's Used Records*, his contract-fulfilling departure from Audium. Its fourteen tracks were all covers and mostly previously issued, on non–Warner Bros. tribute albums (to Webb Pierce, Johnny Cash, Bob Wills, ZZ Top) and one-off projects. Only Dwight's biggest fans would ever know it existed.

As Dwight would later acknowledge, "I tend to have a broader commercial appeal than an Americana label like New West might have realized." Or at least he previously had, when he had the promotional muscle of a major behind him, and he was making music that the major felt it could sell to country radio.

Since the dual trajectory of creativity and commerce had once given Yoakam his stratospheric ascent, it's easy to confuse one with the other after the two veered in different directions. Yoakam's career continued its nosedive in terms of commercial success, one that had begun with the comparative failure in the marketplace of *Gone*, and that Yoakam wouldn't be likely to reverse by going the indie route.

Yet the music itself retained its consistency, its commitment to quality, its adventurous spirit. If anything, Dwight's indie albums were more inspired than his last few albums on a major. And his first album ever to carry the credit "produced by Dwight Yoakam," and first under his deal with New West, is work of which he remains justifiably proud.

At the time, guitarist Keith Gattis had replaced Anderson in Yoakam's band, and Dwight says it was Gattis's suggestion that the artist produce himself rather than inviting someone else. One senses that Yoakam didn't need a whole lot of persuasion.

Whether it was because he was free of Pete or because he had learned so much by working with Anderson, 2005's *Blame the Vain* was both recognizably a Dwight Yoakam album, an extension and continuation of the music he had made for two decades with Pete Anderson, and a liberating experience for its artist-producer. Just as there are cuts here that would have been highlights on any Yoakam album, there are others that reflect the idiosyncrasies of Dwight's personality, independent of Pete, and that would never have appeared on any other Yoakam album.

Fresh and familiar merge on the album-opening title track, where the first fuzz-toned guitar note seems to channel the Beatles tune "I Feel Fine," and then proceeds into a song that Warner Bros. might have been able to promote into a radio hit. It remains a staple of his live performance. At least half of the cuts seem to retain the sound and style that were Yoakam's signature, suggesting that even with a new label and without his producer of two decades, this was still the same artist. These were fastballs, right down the middle.

But what makes the album more interesting are the wicked curves. Just as the early demos demonstrated what Yoakam's music was like before Pete, thus underscoring what sort of focus as a producer and arranger Anderson brought to the picture, Yoakam's first self-produced album shows what his music would be like unyoked from Anderson.

There's an unbridled lack of restraint on a couple of cuts that listeners could dismiss as self-indulgence but which plainly sound like freedom to the artist. The hard-rocking, harmony-laden "International Heartache" tells a tale of a woman scorned who pursues her vengeance with reckless abandon, climaxing with a spoken-word play-by play-that makes a pretty funny song even funnier. Likewise, "She'll Remember" opens with a deadpan comic turn by Dwight in a quasi-British accent, before reverting to honky-tonk shuffle mode.

"We were just fooling around in the studio," explains Yoakam. "And [keyboardist] Skip Edwards was doing this kind of Emerson, Lake, and Palmer synth thing, like 'Lucky Man.' Just to amuse myself, I started playing the clown, with an absurd, stream-of-consciousness in an over-the-top British accent, like Monty Python's interpretation of the Moody Blues. And then drummer Mitch Marine began to play kind of a 'Ticket to Ride' pattern. And it just became part of the track."

A playful, off-the-cuff, in-the-studio part of the track that likely wouldn't have been included with a more regimented, disciplined producer like Pete Anderson. Likewise, the piano break on "Does It Show?" finds Edwards coming closer to evoking Errol Garner (or even Bill Evans) than Floyd Cramer, in an arrangement that exudes the atmospherics of a surreal supper club. The languid "Just Passin' Time" captures a similar feeling, reinforcing the stylistic kinship between Yoakam and California retro-crooner Chris Isaak.

Sandwiched between those two cuts there's "Three Good Reasons," which extends the strategy of "Sorry You Asked" from *Gone*, taking country convention and pushing it to the limits of lyrical absurdity. "I'll give you three good reasons for leavin', and number one is that I've forgotten number two," sings Yoakam. "Number three is in a place that's been kept hidden for so long I can't remember, but it's true."

So there: the Zen koan as country song craft. And a sign that Yoakam was a long way from settling into creative complacency. He never intended this to be the last album of original material he would release. And he still doesn't. Yet, six years later, there has been no more new music from Yoakam.

He insists that the problem isn't lack of material or lack of label options, and that there will be newly recorded original material available in 2012.

In the mean time, let's allow Yoakam to reflect, at length, on how it felt to serve as his own producer. In order to keep this manuscript as timely as possible, Yoakam and I had a long, late phone conversation the week before the book's initial deadline. The experience was so characteristically Dwight—when the time that had been scheduled a full week earlier came for me to call, Dwight was on another line but was "just wrapping up." Call back in fifteen minutes.

Which I did, and Dwight was still "just wrapping up," according to his assistant, who suggested he would call me as soon as he was through. So forty-five minutes later, I received a call from Dwight, who explained that he was still on that conference call (that he'd put on hold), "just wrapping up," but was wondering if it might be better for us to reschedule later in the week. No problem, though the time he spent explaining why we couldn't talk right then and trying to figure out when it would be best for us to talk was longer than many full phone interviews I've conducted.

He finally decided it would be best if he just called me back in an hour. And so he did—two hours later, apologizing profusely for all the delays and complications. But Dwight's mind is itself a complication of wonders. So, here's how producing himself differed from recording with Pete Anderson as producer:

"I think I did some things with EQ differently," he explains. "On *Blame the Vain*, I was doing things with the bass, specifically. The frequency of the bass response was more akin to something you might hear in 1968 than you would in the mid-1970s, when tape heads were wider and you went to twenty-four-track, so you were playing with sonics differently.

"I mean, *Blame the Vain* clearly sounds like one of my records. Pete was always good—the way that Pete and I had worked over the years was that Pete was specifically hired to produce, I didn't demand any co-producing credit, but I signed off on every mix. I went specifically to the mastering lab for each of my albums, starting with *Guitars, Cadillacs*. So, it would have been more different moving from Pete Anderson to a different producer. And I'll still probably co-produce with somebody some day.

"If you listened to *Bridge Over Troubled Water*, which was recorded in like 1971, there was this recording technology that we kind of slipped beyond in the mid-1970s, and everything got overly thick. And we lost the beauty of melody. When we were making *Blame the Vain*, I was talking with David Leonard [who mixed the album] and listening to Connie Francis albums.

"And listening to the Beatles, because Paul McCartney was [initially] a guitar player, and so the way he played bass was different from a lot of quote 'bass players.' And Chris Hillman and I talked about that. In the Byrds he was a mandolin player who wanted to play guitar but got stuck on the bass. He had a hollow body bass because he wanted it to look like a guitar! But that's what made him such a great bass player. You listen to 'Turn, Turn, Turn,' he played with a pick!

"So when we were mixing the *Blame the Vain* album, with Jack White [of the White Stripes], there is no bass! But I love the sound of guitar players who end up being bass players. And when you listen to Simon and Garfunkel, to 'Cecilia' on *Bridge Over Troubled Water*, it has no bass! It has kick drum. So I was in the throes of kind of clearing out the middle. There was just more me, and I was free to experiment.

"Pete and I were both admirers of arrangers, and an acumen for arranging was one of his great gifts, laying out how we were going to arrange tracks, which allowed me to flip paint over my shoulder because of his meticulous attention to detail," he continues.

"For better or worse, having my way with things led to a somewhat different end than previously. I'm a vocalist, so I tend to approach vocals a little more [at a rare loss for words, he pauses here for a good thirty seconds, searching for the right one] *egocentrically*. That would stand to reason, I guess. I don't know in just listening that you would think it was that removed from any other Dwight Yoakam record.

"The more dramatic change was with the Buck album . . ."

21

The Buck Stops Here

BUCK OWENS DIED ON MARCH 26, 2006. Dwight spoke at his memorial service and sang "In the Garden." He had been touring when he received the news, playing a gig in Orlando, Florida. That very day, he and his band began their own personal tribute, performing Buck's songs at sound check, working them up for possible performance or just playing some for their own enjoyment. That *Dwight Sings Buck* would be his next album was inevitable, the only surprise was that Yoakam hadn't attempted such a project earlier in his career, back when he and Pete Anderson were doing their best to emulate Buck Owens and Don Rich.

"I was trying to pay great respect to Buck and that sound and that feel, but to live in the moment for me. It literally took shape at sound checks and onstage after Buck died. So it was born out of the moment I was in, which is how I generally tended to approach what I was doing," Yoakam explains (actually continuing the monologue from the last chapter).

"I'm very proud of the Buck album. I hope it does justice to his memory. I never touched his material before he passed, other than material he brought to me. We weren't mimicking and copying the Buck records. We were making it fresh for 2007. It was really in the spirit of what Buck did. It kind of became its own album; it lived independent of what I was trying to do as a tribute to Buck."

It's an album that takes great liberties with the arrangements, with Yoakam bringing a depth of feeling to vocal performances that rank with his best. You'll hear echoes of the Beatles (who of course had introduced so many '60s rock fans to Buck's "Act Naturally"), the phrasing of Elvis, the Southern rock of the Allman Brothers, the soulfulness of Ray Charles, in Yoakam's musical transformations.

It was as if the songs of Buck Owens contained multiple musical universes, as if everything Dwight loved in music he could hear in Buck. There was no reason to mimic Owens—Buck had already done his own versions to perfection. Dwight and band would have to make the music sound as contemporary and vital as Buck had. Yoakam wanted to renew and extend Buck's musical legacy.

If we permit Dwight to continue his monologue on the recording of the album, here's the way his mind works as far as connecting the dots—in a manner that may often sound like it has nothing to do with his musical tribute to Buck Owens. Or maybe everything.

"In a weird way this was a homage to his late '60s records, were there was bass and drums," he continues. "If you hear 'Here, There and Everywhere,' you realize that *Revolver* changed all of that. In addition to the tape-head size being different and vinyl mastering techniques changing, you also had physically miking techniques that changed with Geoffrey Emerick, a nineteen-year-old who, because he didn't go by the rules, grabbed the kick drum microphone and dragged it to the head of the bass drum. And on *Revolver* stuffed the bass drum full of sweaters. And changed the sound of pop music then and forever, with close miking technique.

"I was always curious about that period of time, '66–'72, the height of great recording technology, the sonics of records in that moment, the arrangers, the Wrecking Crew in L.A. Listen to the band on 'Tambourine Man,' where they wouldn't let anybody [in the Byrds] but McGuinn play. You had great studio bands in New York and L.A. And you look at the band that Chips Moman put together to make Aretha Franklin records.

"And think of the stuff they did, from 'I'm Your Puppet' all the way through to John Prine's first album, when [guitarist] Reggie Young said to John, 'I've been watching you for the last four days, and I'm beginning to think you're either the worst singer-songwriter I've ever heard or the greatest. And I'm starting to think it's the latter.' You had 'Paradise' and 'Sam Stone.'

"And the same band recorded Danny O'Keefe, 'Goodtime Charlie's Got the Blues.' And also, on an off night, when a hippie chick who had come with Mark Lindsey and Paul Revere, because they wanted something of what the Box Tops had, and recorded a little track as a throw off—Merrilee Rush, 'Angel of the Morning.'"

In other words, as the late Donny Hathaway once titled a soul classic, "Everything Is Everything." At least within the mind of Dwight Yoakam, fluid as it is fertile, where Buck, the Beatles, the Byrds, and the Box Tops all share a cosmic connection in the studio, and Paul Revere and the Raiders commingle with John Prine, courtesy of a killer backing band.

"If I had the power, I'd turn back time," he sings with reverence within the hymn-like transformation of the album's "Close Up the Honky-Tonks," but there is no turning back the calendar here. Instead, Yoakam inhabits these songs, some very familiar, many not so (at least to the casual fan), making them his own. His main foil is now Eddie Perez, who had served a stint in the Mavericks, on lead guitar, harmony vocals, even electric sitar. Like Buck had, Dwight recorded the whole album pretty much with his stripped-down studio band, the ones with whom he'd been woodshedding this material at sound checks, finding its edge in live performance.

"Each song began to take on its own shape and expression," writes Yoakam in the liner notes, "and the album became as unique a recording experience as any in my career. It's almost as if Buck was demanding that . . . and, when that happened, it really became our album."

While there necessarily is no new original material on the album, Yoakam by no means sounds like an artist who has run out of creative gas. To the contrary, the labor of love stands as an essential work within Yoakam's recorded output—a milestone of sorts, even a capstone. It seems like it should, by putting an end to one chapter, spark anticipation for the next phase of Yoakam's career, the next great album of original material.

And maybe that will come, though it's now going on five years since Yoakam last released any sort of album, or even had a label affiliation. During the latter stages of recording *Dwight Sings Buck*, he brought in a friend named Laura Mc-Corkindale, to serve as his latest manager. As someone whose résumé extends from entertainment journalist (she had first met Dwight while interviewing him for *Country Music*) to film producer and studio exec, she had no previous management or music industry experience.

But she had Dwight's trust and respect, having negotiated a complicated deal to sell his publishing for a lucrative return. And she had the strong suspicion that Dwight didn't belong on New West, that the indie route had become a commercial dead end for him.

"I very much respected his choice to do *Dwight Sings Buck*, because it was a love letter to a dear, dear friend," says McCorkindale, who didn't officially become his manager until after the album was recorded (but before it was released). "It wasn't a strategically commercial move. It wasn't even an artistically driven choice. It was a choice of the heart, and there's nothing more important in life. But even before I was his manager, I said to him, 'Shouldn't you be with a major label?'"

Though New West still had Dwight under contract, Cameron Strang let him go after *Dwight Sings Buck* with no hard feelings: "An artist like Dwight should do whatever is right for him artistically," he explains. "We never want to be holding somebody up. New West is capable of doing a lot of things, but it has to be a happy marriage. Not that there was any negativity with Dwight, but unless both parties are really committed to a way of doing something in the future, it's going to be really hard to succeed. I think Dwight was ready to try something else."

McCorkindale certainly was. She continues, "New West had some of the most lovable people I've ever worked with, and for an Americana label they're as successful as anybody out there. But Dwight's never been an indie, underground, niche-y artist. So to be with a label like that didn't make a lot of sense to me.

"And after the cycle of *Dwight Sings Buck* ran its course, I suggested pretty damned strongly that it would be impossible for his career to be handled properly being on a label like that. Now some of this is dated, to some degree, because the music business has changed so much since that time. But at the time we were saying, 'Let's be sure this gets nominated for a CMA award or an ACM award,' and no one at the label was even a member [of the leading country music associations]. The mainstream country music business—the Garth Brooks, Shania Twain, Dwight Yoakam country music business—is a very particular business. And it's not New West Records."

These days, it may not even be Garth Brooks, Shania Twain, or especially Dwight Yoakam. But the longer Dwight waits before releasing his next album, the stronger it will need to be in order to re-establish him as a mainstream country star, or to make the world of popular music at large take notice. Because even dating back to his tenure with Warner Bros., Yoakam hasn't been an artist of popular significance since the turn of the century, and hasn't conquered the country charts the way he once routinely did since 1993's *This Time*.

Though his stint with New West found Yoakam flying beneath the radar of mainstream country, both of the two studio albums he recorded there—the last he's released at the time of this writing—stand as career highlights. Whatever promotional support the indie label could or couldn't provide, its support of Yoakam's artistry remained unwavering and absolute.

"Our philosophy at the label was to encourage artists to make as artistic a record as they wanted to make," says Strang. "And the *Dwight Sings Buck* record was an incredible project and so emotionally close to Dwight. He had the freedom to do whatever was in his heart and mind at the moment.

"And the previous record, *Blame the Vain*, was Dwight producing his own album and using his own vision. He makes records that come out of him creatively with so much passion and songwriting presence. So to hear him go from playing the songs on an acoustic guitar to his final production, and all the detail he focuses on, it's really an amazing process. If you love music and the process of making music, he does it right. He's just inspiring to be around."

Yet, in country music, hit singles remain the coin of the realm, and Yoakam's stint at New West failed to produce any, with the music world at large pretty much turning a deaf ear to such inspired artistry as well. Thus, Yoakam now finds himself in almost in the same position as Buck Owens was, gone from the contemporary country scene, a blast from the past, a golden oldie.

Maybe a much younger whippersnapper will do for Dwight what Dwight did for Buck, propel him back into the limelight and onto the charts. Yet in the minds of Dwight, his manager, and those who have heard the music he's been writing, he remains an artist in peak artistic form. He never went away. It's the music business that has disappeared, or at least transformed itself beyond recognition.

22

"I Wanna Love Again, Feel Young Again"

SO, WHAT HAS TAKEN SO LONG?

"Well, have you read the papers?" responds Yoakam with a laugh, his tone suggesting that the very question reeks of cluelessness. "Have you seen *Billboard* magazine? Have you heard the news? *There's no good rockin' tonight.* There's no such thing as records selling. The top-selling album last year, I believe, in the entire record business, was three million units.

"The reason why it's been so long is because of the collapse of the music industry all around us," he continues. "My manager was smart enough to be guarded about pulling the trigger. Believe me, in the last three years, we have begun and stopped several processes of recording an album. I've been writing a lot of material. Going in and recording, and having the budget to put an album together, that we can do. But how do we market music? Where do you sell it?"

The way manager Laura McCorkindale sees it, what seems like a long time—six years and counting since Yoakam's last release of original material, where his longest previous hiatus wasn't half that long—has actually been much shorter than it appears.

"There's no mystery about it," she says. "Look, I've been managing him for four years. The *Dwight Sings Buck* cycle ran a year and a half. Then it took six or seven months for him stewing on the thought I had placed in front of him [to leave New West and return to a major], and another year getting off the label.

"So I came in during a time of a monumental shift in this industry, and this change that we were in the process of going forth with also fell into this weird moment, and then we had to decide what we were going to do," she continues. "The music business world has shifted so much and has continued to shift on a daily or weekly basis. And there were several times when we had made choices about what we were going to do and with whom. And within a few weeks other things popped up that had to be explored. And there have also been a lot of thoughts about the direction of the new music on Dwight's part."

The good news is that there is new music. And there is plenty of it, though Dwight's disappearance from the pipeline of newly recorded material might have led some fans to suspect he'd gone dry, decided to make acting his priority, or was playing out the string as an oldies act on the casino circuit. Increasingly, country music has become a young artist's game. And it's a rare artist in his mid-fifties who can compete against acts less than half that age, particularly when he remains best remembered for hits that are half a lifetime ago.

"I think Dwight's future will be whatever it's meant to be," said Cameron Strang, who left New West in 2011 to become CEO of Warner/Chappell Music (the corporate publishing division) and who has championed Dwight's return to the major label. "And the great thing about Dwight is that he's so true to the art of songwriting and music making, and his knowledge and his roots and his ideas are so entwined and go so deep into the fabric of American music. Like nobody I've ever met.

"And I don't know when popular culture intersects with that sort of artistry to create hit records, but it happened for Dwight, when he was making the *Guitars, Cadillacs* EP, living in an apartment in Hollywood, selling them out of the trunk of his car. And his passion is no different now."

So maybe the odds against Yoakam are no longer than they were for a guy who spent nine years in Los Angeles looking for a break and who somehow skyrocketed from opening act in the roots-punk clubs to the top of the mainstream country charts. And the artist feels younger, creatively at least, than he has in years.

"You know that song 'I Wanna Love Again' on *Blame the Vain*?" he asks. "That was written about my relationship with music. And I wanted to feel like I was fifteen years old again. The song talks about actually having a band, performing live music, or cutting a record, or at sixteen waiting to have the opportunity. That elevated state of excitement about music. It was written like it's a love relationship, but it's really very specifically about that feeling I have for music.

"And it's not easy to get back to that place, that space, where it felt like I was caught up in the youthful exuberance of music. Wanting my musical expression to feel completely free and open, without the tedium of repetition, the familiarity of execution."

Buried toward the end of *Blame the Vain*, the buoyant "I Wanna Love Again" provides a bridge to the material Dwight intends to record. Instead of the brooding, dark Dwight of familiar musical persona—a guy who had to turn to the song-books of Queen and Cheap Trick if he wanted to sing anything positive about love—he has returned from his woodshedding a far sunnier singer-songwriter. And perhaps poppier as well, or at least harder to categorize, in his melodies and arrangements, as traditional country.

"The new music's different," agrees McCorkindale. "It's a bit more universal, even more commercial, without compromising any of his artistry. And he's using his voice in a more open way. Before, a lot of his lyrics were driven by what seemed to be pain. And almost all of his new songs are the opposite. If you put the lyrics to these new songs up against his entire catalog, you would say, 'What changed in his life? Did he get married, did he have kids?' No, no. But there's a hopefulness to this music. Now there is a plethora of love songs."

Strang agrees: "He's played me some songs that he's written and things he's recorded that are as good as anything he's ever done. So there's no decline in Dwight's music. Whatever he does, he's gonna make another great record.

"As to what's popular at the moment, I think it's incredibly healthy for him to be a little bit unhinged from that. You don't want to see somebody chase something that is not who they are—like watching somebody chase after a girlfriend who you know is going to be bad for them."

After Warner Bros. itself spent the spring of 2011 "in play"—with various suitors competing to buy the label—the denouement after the dust settled led Dwight to re-sign with the label that had always given him the creative freedom he needed. Though the production schedule for a book doesn't allow a manuscript to change as quickly as the music industry, Yoakam's management strategy, or Dwight's mind can, there were all sorts of provocative possibilities on the table as this manuscript went to press.

While Warner Bros. Nashville will continue to market Dwight as a country artist to country radio within the country music industry, he had already begun some collaborating with Los Angeles hipster savant Beck (best known for his "Loser" breakout hit) and was exploring the possibility of doing some work with hip-hop-metalhead Kid Rock (who had previously found favor among country fans with "Picture," a duet with onetime Yoakam singing partner Sheryl Crow).

And there was talk that he might co-produce with Joe Chiccarelli, who has established his reputation with acts such as the White Stripes, My Morning Jacket, and the Shins, bands that have been dubbed "indie" or "alternative" but have topped the charts in this topsy-turvy era of music industry upheaval. Warner Bros. Nashville even confirmed much of these details, with a press release dated July 5, 2012. In part, it read:

> "Dwight Yoakam is country music. His voice is immediately recognizable and his artistry is iconic," said John Esposito, Warner Music Nashville's president and CEO. "When I heard his current music, I was blown away. I think that it is some of the best music he has ever done and I'm incredibly proud to have him back at Warner Bros. Records."
>
> Yoakam's highly anticipated new record is set for an early 2012 release and is expected to be co-produced by Joe Chiccarelli (My Morning Jacket, the Shins, the Strokes) along with producer Yoakam, who has recently finished recording several tracks with musician Beck.

Yet the very day after the press release, an e-mail exchange with manager Laura McCorkindale suggested that things had already changed. She cautioned that any mention of Chiccarelli or Beck would be inaccurate by the time the book reaches print, not reflective of the album that Yoakam would record.

She advised that it's "safest to just say Dwight will produce the entire new album himself. And if he brings another person on to do it with him—as I expect—it wouldn't be safe for you to put in print until it's completed anyway. That's January!"

And that's another day in Dwight World, where tomorrow's developments render yesterday's press release obsolete. And six months could see hundreds more changes. In mid-October, at the last possible moment for manuscript revisions, the word was that Dwight was mainly producing and writing alone, although the album would include a cut or two co-produced by Beck and one co-written with Kid Rock. Release was now shifted to early summer, 2012. Stay tuned. It will be interesting to see how much has continued to evolve concerning his studio strategy. What's most significant is that he seems no more likely to adhere to mainstream country formula than he did before his exile from country radio.

In any case, whatever benefits there might be for Dwight to return to a major would seem to be greatest at Warner, which already has such a vested interest in his career, and would reap additional sales of older music from his re-emergence. The same year that Dwight released *Blame the Vain* on New West, Warner Bros. celebrated his illustrious past with the deluxe, twentieth-anniversary expansion of *Guitars, Cadillacs*. The head of the label (not the Nashville division, but the Los Angeles corporate headquarters) when that album was initially issued was Lenny Waronker, who coincidentally had returned to working with the label as a consultant as well as informally advising Dwight.

"He's been godfathering a little bit for me lately, and I'm very grateful," says Yoakam, who treasures the support he received from Warner Bros. when he launched his album with that performance at the Roxy. "After the set, Lenny had said to me, 'You don't know me, other than meeting me last night.

And here's my only advice to you: If anybody at this label ever wants you to do anything that goes against your instinct or intuition, don't listen.'

"Lenny was president of the label then, and he said, 'I'm as proud of everything I ever did with Ry Cooder, Van Dyke Parks, and Randy Newman as I am of Fleetwood Mac. I brought them all to the label, and I'm proud that we have you.' I never received a better piece of advice from a record executive."

As to whatever medium might help the artist and his label take his new music to the marketplace, Yoakam, as always, has been thinking four or five steps ahead. When he left Warner Bros., there'd been talk of him forming his own label. Instead he tried the indie route. Now he sees the future still very much up for grabs.

"I believe the four major labels will always remain, like the four major [movie] studios, as conduits for whatever shape or form delivery of recorded music takes," he says. "I think there'll be CDs for the next three to five years. But I really believe we're entering the age, with satellite radio, which is all I listen to in my car, and with smartphones, that it'll just be streaming. And if it's a stream, we'll monetize it the way songwriters do through BMI or ASCAP, where we're paid for the property we created. Having said that, it seems to be sorting itself out a little more clearly.

"And we're at the point that we're closing in on 200,000 [fans] on Facebook. I do believe that social networking is a good bet. Twitter, I don't think so much. Twitter is very ADD. But Facebook, or whatever's the next incarnation, is a more wholly invested access point for fans. And I think that may be the place for branded artists to continue to interact with their fans."

And make them aware of new music and get them to buy in, whatever form it takes. So as possibilities continue to crystallize with his return to the majors, the future remains wide open. He'd even talked at one point about concentrating on single tracks, downloads, instead of worrying about albums. It's a brave new world for the music industry, or whatever remains of it. And, yet, for Yoakam, the position he finds himself in feels oddly familiar.

"In a strange way, I feel like I'm getting ready for my first album again," he says. "There've been plenty of frustrations with all the delays, arguments with myself, but if it's not right you just have to wait. So in some ways this feels like the nine years in L.A., leading up to finally releasing my first album on Warner Bros."

Could the ascent possibly be as dramatic once again?

Maintains his manager, "Although I'm not fond of the term, I think Dwight is long overdue for a comeback. I think his new album will be incredibly well received. And I think the third act of his artistic career is likely to surpass—commercially and critically—the stunning success that he has had thus far."

Managers are supposed to talk like that, and believe like that, against all odds. But if Dwight can't beat the odds (and I wouldn't necessarily bet against him), and he has to rest on the legacy that he has established thus far, he's already made his mark in musical history. He has accomplished what so many others have attempted—combining country tradition and rock credibility—and none have come anywhere close to achieving on a commercial level that he has. With one foot firmly planted in the country mainstream and the other just as firmly in alt-country, roots-rock progressivism, Dwight stands alone, straddling two worlds that otherwise don't have much to do with each other.

Let's leave the last word to Chris Hillman, the most country-minded compatriot of Gram Parsons in the Byrds, and the co-founder with Parsons of the Flying Burrito Brothers (as well as co-writer of much of that band's material). The late Parsons remains revered as the embodiment of this sort of music, a seminal force in the merging of country and rock, but Hillman maintains that what Parsons merely promised, Yoakam has delivered.

"[Gram] could have been a Dwight Yoakam, but Dwight worked real hard," he says (in *Hot Burrito: The True Story of the Flying Burrito Brothers*, written by John Einarson with Hillman). "Gram didn't. Dwight had the drive, the focus, the work ethic, and the professionalism. Gram had none of that."

Yet there have been so many books analyzing and celebrating Parsons's artistry, impact, aura, and legacy. Now there's one on Yoakam.

The Dwight Dozen

A Selected Discography

Guitars, Cadillacs, Etc., Etc. (EP, Oak, 1984; LP, Reprise, 1986; Deluxe Edition, Reprise/Rhino, 2006): One title, three incarnations. The best place to start is the Deluxe Edition, which documents the development that led to his breakthrough and lays the foundation for everything that followed.

Hillbilly Deluxe (Reprise, 1987): Now an established mainstream country star, Dwight avoids the sophomore slump with a follow-up as strong as the debut.

Buenas Noches from a Lonely Room (Reprise, 1989): The artistry matures (and darkens), as Dwight brings Buck Owens back to the "Streets of Bakersfield" and the top of the country charts.

If There Was a Way (Reprise, 1990): Dwight's first attempt at Nashville co-writing reaps the benefits of collaborations with Roger Miller and Kostas.

This Time (Reprise, 1993): A popular breakthrough well beyond country. His best-selling album and arguably his best.

Dwight Live (Reprise, 1995): The live-wire charge shows how Dwight distinguishes himself onstage from the mainstream country pack, while the homage to Elvis Presley is more explicit than ever.

Gone (Reprise, 1995): A big creative leap results in a commercial downturn. This is the most polarizing album of Dwight's career.

A Long Way Home (Reprise, 1998): As the title suggests, the music returns full circle.

dwightyoakamacoustic.net (Reprise, 2000): Dwight's artistry distilled to its essence: voice, songs, acoustic guitar.

Population: Me (Koch/Audium, 2003): Dwight takes the indie route on the last album with producer Pete Anderson riding shotgun.

Blame the Vain (New West, 2005): Dwight's first self-produced album and his last to feature original material (for six years and counting).

Dwight Sings Buck (New West, 2007): An inevitable and inspired tribute to Dwight's late mentor, followed by the longest hiatus of Dwight's recording career.

To be continued . . .

Acknowledgments

WORKING WITH DWIGHT YOAKAM made this a rich and re-velatory adventure, an opportunity to immerse myself in not only his music but also his monologues (as interviews with Dwight quickly become). He attached no strings to his coop-eration, neither asking for nor receiving any editorial control. He said more than once that he appreciated the interest a uni-versity press was showing in his artistry.

Though I recognize and respect the distinction between music journalism and fandom, I don't think it's possible to be an effective critic without retaining a fan's passion for music. After two years, I'm even more of a fan of Yoakam's music, more convinced of the singularity of his achievement, than I was when I began this project.

As Yoakam's manager, Laura McCorkindale not only served as gatekeeper to Dwight, but as a valuable resource in her own right, providing context and insight, as well as contacts for others involved with Yoakam's career. She balanced a manager's protective instincts with a former journalist's nose for a good story. In fact, one of her early concerns was that Yoakam might one day want to write his own story, and she didn't want this to compromise his publishing prospects. From talking with Dwight, I know that we just scratched the surface, and I eagerly anticipate reading the Joycean memoir he might compose.

As co-founder of *No Depression*, Peter Blackstock served as my editor at that late, lamented publication, and he was my friend and fellow music journalist in Austin well before then. Peter's talks with the University of Texas Press generated this project. He also provided a typically astute first reading of the manuscript for editorial review. I trust that Peter and I will continue to work together, and I look forward to it.

I value the commitment and the patience that the University of Texas Press has shown throughout my dealings with them. I had most frequent contact with sponsoring editor Allison Faust and manuscript editor Victoria Davis, and I would like to thank them in particular, as well as all others at UT Press who have been involved in the acquisition, editing, production, and promotion of this book. It takes a village . . .

In the critical final stages, copy editor Laura Griffin brought a fresh eye and keen instincts to the manuscript, saving me from embarrassment, imprecision, and repetition. Any flaws that remain are, of course, my fault.

Since I originally conceived of this as a critical biography of Dwight's music—with more analysis than reporting—I wasn't sure at the outset how much interviewing I might do. But even before Dwight agreed to talk with me, I knew that I needed context from those who had discovered and supported his talent before his recorded music could tell its own story. Bill Bentley and Dave Alvin were both early and crucial sources, ones who gave this project a big boost, just as each had given Dwight during those critical early stages of his career.

Pete Anderson proved a key participant, invaluable in the perspective he provided, as I tried to sort out how the Yoakam-Anderson collaboration had worked, who did what, why it became so successful, how it fell apart. As with Dwight, I wasn't sure when I began this project whether Pete would talk with me (and since I hadn't read anything since their split in which either discussed the other, I figured silence might be part of a legal settlement). But he was gracious with his time and generous with his reflections, never attempting to settle grudges or grind axes. It was partly because Pete figured so heavily, prominently, and repeatedly in Dwight's own telling of his story that Pete's voice proved all the more necessary to this project.

Pete's recording partner Dusty Wakeman also provided a unique perspective, simultaneously inside the studio and outside the Yoakam-Anderson collaborative relationship. Another significant interviewee with a dual vantage was Cameron Strang, whose perspective proved pivotal after his move from New West to Warner/Chappell Music predated Dwight's return to the Warner family. As related in the book, one of the delightful detours this project took was my impromptu exchange with Jim Ed Norman, in which the head of Warner Bros. Nashville during Dwight's heyday there talked at length (and, ultimately for publication) about why he was reluctant to participate.

And it was serendipity that I had the opportunity to chat with Steve Earle and Joe Ely on successive days as a result of different assignments, and to pick the brains of each concerning Dwight. (A funny coincidence: I had written a Sunday *Chicago Sun-Times* arts section cover feature in the mid-1980s focusing specifically on these three as signs of country insurgence and creative vitality, and now here we all were, a quarter of a century later.)

I'd known from the start that I would augment my own account of Dwight's musical development with passages from other journalists. All of those sources have been credited within the text, but I would particularly like to thank John Rumble, senior historian for the Country Music Hall of Fame and Museum, whose assistance with the archives in Nashville helped focus what might have otherwise become a fishing expedition. In particular, the transcript from one of Dwight's earliest interviews, with Paul Kingsbury (October 18, 1985), is courtesy of the Frist Library and Archive of the Country Music Hall of Fame.

Speaking of fishing expeditions, I sent Jackie Witkowski on one, when I was swamped with school responsibilities during this project's earliest stages, and she proved a most valuable research assistant by finding a slew of pertinent articles with minimal direction from me. One of the great things about teaching at the University of Iowa is having great students to draw upon.

The University of Iowa School of Journalism and Mass Communication additionally provided resources and moral support (along with steady employment), and Dr. David Perlmutter helped me secure a research fund from the College of Liberal Arts and Sciences, enough to subsidize short trips to Los Angeles and Nashville.

Of all the journalists who have written over the decades about Dwight, two whose work I found particularly helpful were Holly George-Warren (her notes to Dwight's four-disc compilation and the deluxe edition of his debut) and Patrick Carr (his series of provocative profiles for *Country Music*).

My good friends Lloyd Sachs and John Soss have spent decades experiencing this music (and plenty of other music) with me. John read a pivotal chapter early on, and Lloyd read the whole manuscript toward the end, each providing valuable feedback and support. Through all these years of sharing and listening, both have helped shaped my musical thinking in ways that go well beyond Dwight Yoakam.

As always, my preoccupation throughout the project required the patience of my family, so greatest thanks go to Maria and Molly McLeese and to Kelly Youland (who capped this project by getting a doctoral degree, a residency, a husband, and a new name during the weeks immediately before this manuscript was due). Everything I write is for them, and they have continued to bless my life beyond anything I deserve.